opening
your child's
spiritual windows

Also by Cheri Fuller

opening your child's spiritual windows

Ideas to Nurture Your Child's Relationship with God

cheri fuller

Author of *Opening Your Child's Nine Learning Windows*

ZondervanPublishingHouse
Grand Rapids, Michigan

A Division of HarperCollinsPublishers

Opening Your Child's Spiritual Windows
Copyright © 2001 by Cheri Fuller
Requests for information should be addressed to:

▣ZondervanPublishingHouse
Grand Rapids, Michigan 49530

Library of Congress Cataloging-in-Publication Data
Fuller, Cheri.
    Opening your child's spiritual windows : ideas to nurture your child's relationship
with God / Cheri Fuller.
      p. cm.
    Includes bibliographical references.
    ISBN 0-310-22449-7
    1. Christian education of children.   2. Children—Religious life.   3. Spiritual life—
Christianity.   I. Title.

BV1475.2 .F86 2001
248.8'45—dc21
                                                 2001017806

Interior design by Melissa Elenbaas

Printed in the United States of America

---

01 02 03 04 05 06 /❖ DC/ 10 9 8 7 6 5 4 3 2 1

To our grandson,
Caleb Cole Fuller,
born October 30, 2000

contents

acknowledgments

Special thanks go to Greg Johnson, my agent, for his creativity, support, and vision for this project. Thanks to Sandy Vander Zicht, my editor, and the wonderful team at Zondervan. My appreciation also goes to Shenae Nicholson, Jessica Monzo, and Connie Willems for assistance in innumerable ways, to Pete Hohmann, Diane DuBose, and Patty Armstrong for sharing resources, and to all the parents who shared stories about their children.

Heartfelt thanks to all the marvelous kids I've worked with through the years, to the children at Bridgeway Church in Oklahoma City—especially the Prayer Class kids who teach *me* so much—and to the children I work with at the Jimmy Everest Center at Children's Hospital, who inspire me week after week with their incredible courage as they battle cancer and leukemia.

I am always grateful for my family, especially my husband, Holmes, for his constant support and prayers, our children (I've learned the most from you!) and their spouses—Justin and Tiffany, Chris and Maggie, Alison and Hans—and our grandchildren—Caitlin, Caleb, and a little Plum on the way—who are the greatest blessings in our lives this side of heaven.

The child's "house has many mansions"—
including a spiritual life that grows, changes,
responds constantly to the other lives that, in their
sum, make up the individual we call by a name and
know by a story that is all his, all hers.

—Robert Coles,
The Spiritual Life of Children

You have made us for yourselves
and our hearts are restless until
we find our rest in you.

—St. Augustine

Children are natural seekers;
they just need us to point the way.

—Karen Henley,
Child-Sensitive Teaching

one

spiritual windows

Pathways to the Heart

When our first child was delivered into our arms, it was obvious that he was very vocal and expressive with his emotions, both positive and negative. Extremely active, Justin tuned up his lungs nightly to protest being confined in his high chair at dinnertime. At only eighteen months old, he exuberantly climbed up onto the roof at the first sight of a ladder. If he saw something he wanted from a top cabinet, even the off-limits medicine shelf, he persistently climbed up again and again. Now in his twenties and still adventurous, he recently completed a rugged fifty-mile trail run.

When his little brother, Chris, came on the scene almost three years later, we couldn't believe how different the two boys were. Chris was calm and happy. He was entertained by quietly observing the mobile in his crib or by watching the dog swish her tail in the family room. Resourceful and creative, Chris could be content whether he was playing with other kids or making his own fun.

Alison, our daughter, lit up our lives two and a half years later. The pediatrician's first words right after Alison's delivery proved prophetic: "She's one of the feistiest babies I've checked in years! Alison won't be a doormat; she has plenty of spunk—which I think she'll need with two big brothers." Sure enough, our precious daughter held her own with her older brothers and stood up to the kindergarten class bully. Yet if anyone was hurting, she was the first to comfort that person. At only five years old, she said, "I'll do my hair myself, Mom," and she did.

Our three children are also wired with different ways of learning about the world around them, and naturally, each is endowed with unique gifts. Justin has tremendous communication and "people" skills, and he gravitated to history, English, and later, business and marketing. He now serves as an account manager for a surgical equipment company. His brother, Chris, took every science course offered, majored in humanities, and went on to medical school after college. Alison, a hands-on learner, had foreign language talent and mastered information best when she got involved in doing, making, or experimenting. Enormously creative, she designed her own greeting cards, and when she found an ad for an art school in fourth grade, she inquired, "Could I just drop out of regular school and go to this art school in St. Louis instead?" She's now working part-time as a hair stylist while attending college and expecting her first child.

Our children's spiritual journeys have been just as individual. While all three of our kids grew up in the same churches and heard the same *Little Visits with God* devotions and Bible stories at home, their growth in knowing and walking with God has been quite different. Spiritual growth happened on their own timetables.

Alison, our youngest, had a very real encounter with Jesus in seventh grade. But while she helped lead worship for youth group from junior high on and taught a girls' Bible study, she struggled to believe and wrestled with doubts. Alison always loved God but didn't like religion, rules, and things that alienated people outside the church. The only thing that motivated her in her faith was the example Jesus set—not a doctrine from a denomination or church but how he touched people no matter their brokenness or outward appearance. Her faith became real in her early twenties after she challenged everything she'd been taught when she was young.

Older brother Justin attended church throughout childhood, but in adolescence he found the party scene at his high school much more interesting than youth group. He wanted his faith to be his own and, until then, wasn't interested in borrowing ours. But at the end of his sophomore year of college, he got tired of the emptiness and stress of living life without God and realized God hadn't moved— Justin had. He had a definite spiritual turnaround and has followed the Lord ever since. Now he is the father of two young children, praying with and for them, wanting to teach them in such a way that they'll know Christ and be able to touch others' lives with his love, and endeavoring to reflect Jesus in the corporate world where he works, whether that means praying for someone or listening to them.

Chris was the first to profess his faith in Christ, as a nine-year-old, and continued attending church with us and mandatory chapel services at the private high school he attended. His analytical nature, however, caused him to doubt the Bible when it didn't line up with scientific knowledge he was learning. College provided the opportunity to explore conflicts and contradictions of religion apparent to Chris as he struggled to make sense of the shared yet remarkably varied human experience. As he sifted through the theories, stories, and worldviews accumulated throughout cultures and ages, a personal conviction emerged which was not memorized from a lecture on "isms" or learned from a Sunday school workbook.

Chris discovered the *actions* of Jesus and made Christ the cornerstone for a life of affecting the world in a powerful, compassionate, and humble way. He found that faith and empowerment through Jesus, realized in a deeply personal and individual sense, enables his quest to touch people's hearts, improve their condition, and perhaps leave the fingerprint, rather than the academics, of God in their lives.

For decades, psychologists have debated whether children are born with a clean personality slate or whether much of their basic makeup has already been determined. My husband and I have debated the issue as well. Just when we would get one of our kids figured out and on the right path, one of the others would completely baffle us. The reason? God made each of them unique. Someone said raising kids is like nailing Jell-O to a tree; we have plans for our kids and are ready to nail them down when suddenly—oops! Slosh! There goes the child with a will of his own, sliding down a path different from what we'd envisioned. Maybe it's God's way of keeping us parents on our toes—and on our knees in prayer.

As psychologists debate such issues, so theologians debate the spiritual development of children. Why do some "catch it" early in life and others not "get it" until their twenties or thirties? Why do some run toward God and others run as far away from him as they can? Is it a function of "strong willed" versus "compliant"? Will children be stronger spiritually if the husband is the spiritual leader, or if the wife is? Or does the influence of a praying, involved grandparent really make the difference? Is it the pastor? The youth minister? The style of worship? Christian schooling?

The variables are legion.

Just as children have critical windows of opportunity for learning language, music, and logic, as my book *Opening Your Child's Nine Learning Windows* discusses, they also have important spiritual windows of opportunity. These windows are pathways to your children's hearts during their growing-up years, when their hearts and minds are most open to experiencing the wonder of God's creation, coming to know him and his ways through the Bible, talking and listening to him through prayer, serving him, and participating in the church community. These windows are best opened early in life, though as you'll discover, if a child's personality or circumstances keep her from a specific stage in the process, any time in life can be the right time to catch up.

It's essential, however, that a parent start early. Why? The early years are the time when children are most receptive to spiritual nurturing and training. According to Dr. Robert Coles, a child psychiatrist who spent over twenty-five years studying the spiritual life of children, kids spend a lot of time thinking and wondering about God, pondering questions like, "What are we?" "Who made us?" and "What are we here for?" As he explains, they are natural seekers, as eager to make sense of life as we adults are. They are seekers marching through life with an important mission and spiritual purpose.[1]

The first six years are important because children are most open then to encounters with God and the enjoyment they derive from those experiences, says Sofia Cavalletti, a pioneer in spiritual formation.[2] Because they are more contemplative in early childhood and more inclined toward intellectual and moral interests in later childhood, it is a critical time for spiritual development. Moreover, studies show that 85 percent of kids' attitudes about God, church, and the Bible develop in the preschool years. And the fact that the vast majority of people who follow a Christian lifestyle received Christ between the ages of four and fourteen reveals the importance of nurturing a child's spirit early in life.[3]

Young children are seekers and have a God-shaped vacuum inside just as we adults do. As parents, we have the awesome privilege of leading them to the only one who can fill that vacuum. "The most excellent end for which we were created is that one should teach another about God, what He is in His being, what His will is, how He is minded towards us," said Martin Luther.

A Perspective on Spiritual Development

While I'm aware of theories on the spiritual development of children and include explanations of several in the appendix, I don't rely heavily on such theories in this book for two reasons. First, in the majority of cases, adults tend to underestimate the enormous spiritual capacity of children. Children, even at a very young age, have much more potential to know God and connect with him, listen to him, and have a relationship with him than we imagine (or sometimes than even we can experience ourselves). So we can't presuppose that just because preschoolers are in the phase Piaget describes as magic or fantasy, their ideas about God are in the realm of pretend play and they're too young to really experience God. Or that it's only teenagers who think through what people have told them throughout their lives about God. Or that kids can serve God only after they've gotten a lot of Bible knowledge and gone to seminary or college.

The second reason is that each child is unique, so a cookie-cutter approach to spiritual development would be erroneous. Every person's spiritual path is different. Most spiritual development occurs in the heart where we can't measure the progress. God sees the heart, and we see just the outside, the external person. A child or teen can seemingly be in a spiritual slumber for years and then, in a matter of a few days or weeks, speed ahead in spiritual growth. As much as we'd like to, we can't control the acceleration and we can't force it. For the most part, spiritual journey and development are a mystery.

Just as one child may be one to three years ahead of another child of the same age in language development or physical development, so a child's spiritual development can be fast or slow. There are many variables: the spiritual foundation in the home; the love or lack of it in the child's early life; what his life, family, and church experiences have been; whether there have been encounters with death, struggles which have propelled him to ask hard questions and search out meaning, or traumatic events that derailed him from his path or caused him to draw back from God.

Fortunately, God is not keeping track of who reaches what stages of spiritual growth the fastest. He doesn't face the pressure parents put on themselves to make sure their child is born again before she graduates from high school. And he's not giving out ribbons and prizes for the spiritual sprinters or putting the spiritual slow learners in the corner. His view of the playing field is bigger, so he is extremely patient. His ultimate mission is to draw children to his heart and show them that he loves them with an everlasting love. He longs to have an intimate relationship with them, to live through them and have them abide in him, and ultimately, to mold them into the image of Christ.

For these reasons, I have approached spiritual development in a different way. I've discovered that healthy spiritual progress occurs when the child is helped through a series of key spiritual windows.

Spiritual Windows

Spiritual windows are opportunities for the heart to grasp the true nature of God and what it means to live the Christian life. They are different from the opportunities provided by Christian education or sports. As helpful as a good education is, it may provide only the facts of God and the Bible without touching the "my heart to God's heart" that must happen to make strong followers of Christ. These are windows of the heart, and they are perhaps the most important ones we need to open. And as great as sports are for fitness and self-esteem, they don't teach the timeless truths that will lead children to the Savior.

As Jim Cymbala says in his book *Fresh Faith,* our children's spiritual nurture is far more important than mere material things or anything else we can do for our kids: "Did you know that parents can feed their children three nutritious meals a day and put the latest $120 sneakers on their feet and still deprive them spiritually? To withhold from children the knowledge of the wonderful and loving God who created them is the worst kind of parenting. They cannot truly live without Jesus, regardless of the top-drawer education they might receive."[4]

If we want our kids to learn a sport someday, we may get them a football or basketball. We throw the ball in the yard and encourage them to play. As soon as possible, we take them to lessons or team practice, making sure they have the best coach we can find. We want them to learn the basics. So we practice with them and often watch their lessons and drills, buy them equipment, and encourage them to stick with it! We may send them to a special basketball camp in the summer to gain additional skills. Later we cheer from the stands when they're on the playing field.

This support, teaching, and encouragement in our children's lives as they develop the skills and confidence to participate, compete, or perform in a sport is invaluable, an important part of our parenting. But this won't necessarily guarantee that they'll have the heart to make it to the highest levels of that sport—a love for it has to be built. As a basketball shoe commercial asked years ago, "Do you got the love?"

The greatest privilege we have as parents is to help our children "get the love" for God and for living the Christian life. As a coach nurtures young athletes, so we must focus on the spiritual nurture of our kids. This means bringing them to Jesus, modeling a vibrant, joyful Christian life of service they'll want to follow, mentoring them in prayer, teaching them how God's Word can guide their lives, and rejoicing as they grow up spiritually. I heard a pastor one Sunday say, "What will it profit a man if he gain the whole world, but forfeit his own son?" He was saying that if we or our children succeed in the world's eyes, but fail in the Lord's eyes, what good has any of it been?

The church can't do it for us. It can help; it can reinforce what children are learning in the home. But the church isn't the primary delivery source for the Christian faith–home and family are. We can't leave the spiritual nurturing to Barney or Teletubbies or even *VeggieTales* videos (as wonderful and fun as those resources are). It's a job especially created for parents.

It's not the intention of this book to be *the* definitive work on what guarantees the proper spiritual development of your child. But in my experience as a parent, teacher, researcher, children's ministry leader, and grandmother, I am convinced of some general trends. Namely, that just as each learning window is a building block for greater levels of intelligence and creativity, there are spiritual windows children pass through in order to build a faith in Christ that lasts.

A faith that lasts.

This is what every Christian parent wants for his or her child. A secure eternity is the obvious goal, but so is the abundant life that Jesus promises in John 10:10: "Life in all its fullness" (LB).

How do you get there from here? By opening your child's spiritual windows at the appropriate time, in a loving, sensitive way. Cultivating your child's spiritual progress is not done overnight. That's why this book is a training manual, a resource for the long haul, offering you the abstract areas of your child's spiritual needs, then giving the concrete how-to's in meeting them. And if you are a new Christian or are not very far along on your spiritual journey, don't fret. You can grow with your children. As you nurture their spiritual life, you'll grow as well. In fact, all parents must nurture their own spiritual life so that the example of lifetime growth is exemplified early and often.

Components of This Book

In each chapter of this book, you'll find true-life stories and creative activities in the "Making the Most" section–ranging from role-playing a Bible story, to observing zoo animals, building a birdhouse, and spotting the Milky Way–all with the purpose of opening your child's spiritual windows. Though I have suggested appropriate age ranges for each of these activities, you can adapt them for a wide range of ages, and with a parent's help, many activities can be done with younger children. For some activities, I'll highlight special points and ways to adapt these activities for preschoolers, elementary kids, or teens.

Since open communication between parent and child is the core of a lasting relationship, the questions and prompts included in each chapter in the "Heart to Heart" sidebars will serve as a springboard for you to share with your child from *your* life, ideas, and spiritual journey. The Scripture quotations will point you to what God's Word has to say about the particular spiritual window, and the "Journal Jots" will show you ways to encourage your child to write about her experiences with God. When you write about something, you learn it better. These journal opportunities are great for any family, and if you're a homeschool parent, you could integrate them into your regular school day. A journal can become a lifelong companion as your child writes her questions, thoughts, ideas, and prayers, as well as the most important markers in her spiritual journey. If your child can't write yet, she can dictate responses to you, or you can postpone this activity until she's older. The child's resource list, called "Bookworm," supplies kids with good reading material pertinent to each chapter's topic, for a wide range of ages and in various genres. In addition, I include books and helpful resources for parents in the "Bookshelf" sidebar.

What are the spiritual windows we want to open in our child's life? I'm going to discuss four primary big picture windows, and each of these has other windows inside them.

1. Enjoying God
2. Loving God
3. Following God
4. Serving God

Each window leads to the next one. Though age does not necessarily matter, our natural parental desire is for our children to get to number four—Serving God—as early in life as possible. Getting there, however, means not skipping any of these essential stages. If you examine these chapters carefully, comparing the principles with your own experience and that of Christians you've known, you'll likely discover that if one window was missed, the result was often spiritual stagnation and (too often) unhealthy concepts about God and living the Christian life.

You have the ability to influence, nurture, and shape your child's spiritual development. You—and the other adults God puts in your child's life—can either open or close these windows. So join in as we pursue an understanding of the first window—the Enjoying God Window.

part one

enjoying God

You may wonder, Why do we start with the topic of enjoying God? Isn't that a more advanced spiritual skill reserved for mature Christians who've served on the mission field most of their lives or for high-profile pastors and leaders who've studied the Bible in seminary?

The Enjoying God Window is our beginning place because the early years are the prime time for naturally enjoying God. In other words, children actually have a greater innate capacity to enjoy God than adults do. As Sofia Cavalletti, a pioneer in children's spiritual formation, observes, "Indeed, we believe that early childhood is the time of the serene enjoyment of God when the response [the child] gives to God consists in the very acceptance of the gift in fullness of joy."[1]

There will come a time for spiritual disciplines, for a different response based on thinking through the Scriptures, questioning, serving, and owning one's spiritual journey. But for young children, relationship with God can somehow exist mysteriously on a plane of trusting faith—what we often term "childlike faith."

Since you are the major influence in your child's spiritual life, the first chapter in part 1 is addressed to you and your relationship with God. It includes some ideas and suggestions to help you start enjoying God if you are not already enjoying his presence in your life. For as you begin enjoying God, the natural by-product is that you will naturally pass that enjoyment on to your child.

As you'll see in the Wonder Window and Worship Window chapters that follow, you don't have to stop enjoying God as you grow up or leave him behind with your Star Wars backpack from elementary school. God wants us to enjoy him, not just as kids, not just as adults, but *forever*.

You need to continually ensure that the love bond in your family is strong. Without that, children will react to parental guidance and especially spiritual guidance, with resentment and hostility.

—Ross Campbell, M.D.,
Relational Parenting

Actually, the spiritual reality a child needs begins in the heart of the parents. . . . That "Mom and Dad first" approach is where spiritual reality begins, according to the Bible. You cannot give what you yourself do not have, and you cannot lead a child where you have not been. . . . The spiritual reality every child needs to find at home is, first and foremost: a relationship, not a religion.

—Ron Hutchcraft,
Five Needs Your Child Must Have Met at Home

The home should be a self-contained shelter of security; a kind of school where life's basic lessons are taught; a kind of church where God is honored.

—Billy Graham

two

the **enjoying God**
window

My friend Joanna grew up in a loving home, and her parents were fun people. She enjoyed their company, even—believe it or not—during her adolescent years. Joanna's family spent time together, laughed together, and took trips together. Her parents were there to cheer Joanna on at every stage of growing up: at spelling bees, as she performed at football games, as she got her physical therapy degree, and later as she walked down the aisle and married. Because of this history, Joanna admits her parents were always easy to love. That doesn't mean there were never squabbles or tensions, but Joanna knew, without a shadow of a doubt, that she was loved and that her parents could be trusted. And when there were problems, they talked things through and worked them out.

As Joanna grew up and her parents got older, they went right on enjoying each other. She related to her parents in the right way for the right reasons. They'd built a strong relationship that lasted a lifetime, and that gave her a desire to serve them when her dad had a heart attack and when her mom went through health problems and depression after a series of personal losses.

Like you, perhaps, I remember a childhood friend whose parents were mean and rather controlling. Sally still loved her parents, though most of the time it was out of fear. It was a dysfunctional love that got stuck in the fear stage and never advanced to mutual enjoyment. Her parents were too busy with their careers to spend much time with her. The children followed their parents' directions and orders, at least for a time, but never progressed to deeper stages of relationship with their parents. In college the kids would often feel they were being manipulated or controlled when a barrage of advice came regarding what major to choose or what to become. They began to distance themselves from home. In fact, when they grew up and could make their own decisions, they moved as far away from their parents as possible.

> You will show me the
> path of life;
> In Your presence is
> fullness of joy;
> At Your right hand are
> pleasures forevermore.
>
> —PSALM 16:11 nkjv

Healthy homes create enjoyment, which can develop into love. Because Joanna loved her parents, she obeyed them (most of the time). And her love for them led her to follow most of their basic values and to serve them in the little things kids do to help their parents. Sally never enjoyed her parents; she loved them only because of the blood tie, obeyed out of fear, and consequently, will likely never willingly serve them when they need her the most.

Faith Transition

Sadly, I don't know too many adults who enjoy, love, obey, and serve God the way Joanna did her parents.

I've met thousands of evangelicals, charismatics, and mainline churchgoers in my last twenty years of ministry. Unfortunately, it is rare to find a Christian who *truly enjoys God* and who's loving, obeying, and serving him because they've experienced so much pleasure and delight in their relationship. Yet that is the chief end for people—to enjoy and love God now and forever![2] That's not to say few people have ever enjoyed God. Most people at one time in their life had a sense of joy at being one of his children and felt accepted in his presence. But they've misplaced the joy or confused obedience and service for enjoyment. The result is a faith by memory and rote rather than a faith of wonder and love. It's not unlike what happens to some children and parents who've had a difficult time together.

When Kevin was very young, his natural tendency was to love his parents freely. His mom and dad returned that love. But when he started asserting his will, disobedience followed. Discipline, especially poorly administered discipline, often put a wedge in the relationship. As he grew older and the rebellion got more serious, tougher discipline often followed. Deeper wedges were formed. The result: Kevin lost the wonder of the relationship, didn't want to obey, and consequently, rarely attempted to deepen the child-parent bond. Instead, he escaped.

> Draw near to God and He will draw near to you.
>
> —JAMES 4:8 nkjv

During college and his early single years, he came back at holidays out of a sense of obligation. He continues to call his parents Mom and Dad on rare occasions, but the thought that he could enjoy his relationship with his parents disappeared years ago. During an honest moment, the parents would probably say the same. They don't have to say, "I don't enjoy you and won't spend time with you"; they simply show it by their actions.

Does this sound like anyone you know as it relates to their relationship with God? They'll visit God at Christmas and Easter but aren't in any way motivated to enjoy him. I know dozens of Christians in the same relational position, but they don't have the courage to quit the Sunday routine. They show up every week out of duty or habit but have no more interest in enjoying God than the holiday attender. It's social, convenient, "good for the kids"—but the thought of relishing a relationship with their Creator is long gone.

> Be still, and know that I am God.
>
> —PSALM 46:10

I've learned the hard way that you can't take your children any farther than you are yourself. There were years that I didn't enjoy

God. Oh, I went to church on Sunday. But I wasn't spending time with God or trusting him; I wasn't loving God with all my heart—which is the number one commandment. I'd been disappointed with God's handling of things ever since my father, grandfather, aunt, and a close schoolmate died within a few short years of each other. My heart was disconnected from God because of my perception that God is unjust; I experienced spiritual stagnation instead of growth. Since I was convinced God couldn't be trusted, I began living life my way. For me, this eventually led to feeling empty and discouraged about where my life was going.

> Because Your lovingkindness is better than life, My lips shall praise You.
>
> —PSALM 63:3 nkjv

It was only as I began to rekindle a childhood faith and to experience God's love as a twenty-nine-year-old that I started growing spiritually. Not surprisingly, I was soon able to share God's goodness and love with my kids, to talk with them about the tough questions, to pray with them, and to truly make them feel welcome in God's presence. I desired to live the way the Bible instructed, and more than anything else, I wanted to serve him with my whole heart.

Two Priorities to Start

The truth is, *you* must first enjoy God; otherwise your children probably won't. And second, if you don't have a loving, trusting relationship with your children, they will tend to reject or miss much of the influence your spiritual life could have on them.

The starting place for opening your child's spiritual windows is nurturing your own relationship with Christ and your relationship with your child. As Dr. Bruce Wilkinson says, "It's interesting—the same moment we choose to fulfill God's desire in our family by producing godly offspring, God immediately redirects our focus from our children to us, their parents!"[3]

Your family—and the church family—has about eighteen years to build a sense of wonder and enjoyment of God into your child. How well are we accomplishing this mission? Personally, given what I see of the people and leaders in churches, coupled with the drop-out rate of teenagers who graduate from high school and promptly graduate from God, I'd say we have a way to go. This book isn't about criticizing the church. It's about looking to the future and making the changes necessary to open your child's spiritual windows—and keep them open!

People Have Their Reasons

There are many reasons why you might not enjoy God:

- You don't know God. If you've never spent time with God, if you've never gotten to know him or be with him, how can you enjoy him? You can't enjoy somebody you don't know.
- You have wrong perceptions about God or about yourself. Or perhaps you've believed lies about God from our culture. Lies about God—such as he doesn't really care about you, is always angry with you, or doesn't love you—keep you from enjoying him. Other lies may include: he's not relational, he's not for you, he may be good to other people but not to you. If you truly believe God is angry or mean, why would you want to spend quiet time with him?
- Your past experiences have taught you that you can't trust God. You've been hurt at one time and think he's the cause. Maybe you've been disappointed with God, and it's hard to enjoy someone you don't trust or are disappointed in. You

> Come, all you who are thirsty, come to the waters;
> and you who have no money, come, buy and eat!
> Come, buy wine and milk without money and without cost.
> Why spend money on what is not bread, and your labor on what does not satisfy?
> Listen, listen to me, and eat what is good, and your soul will delight in the richest of fare.
>
> —ISAIAH 55:1–2

may never have been shown a positive picture of God. Perhaps your earthly father was harsh or unloving and you transferred that picture to God.

- You're caught up in misplaced affections and misplaced priorities, perhaps filling the void in your life with work, ambition, money and material things, children, sports, and a myriad of things in this world. To spot misplaced affections, ask, "What is it I think about most? What consumes my life and my imagination?"

> Be glad and rejoice forever in that which I create.
>
> —ISAIAH 65:18 rsv

- You're distracted. Even if at one time you enjoyed God during an inspiring worship service or while observing the Atlantic Ocean from the beach, life is going too fast; you're in a whirlwind of activity and so distracted that the thought of a quiet time to enjoy God seems impossible. The busyness of most people's lives—especially parents'—is staggering. It's easy for us to get caught in the whirlwind of everyday living. This was the case for a mom who came up to me after a message I shared on prayer and wept, "I'm too frantically busy and overwhelmed with carpooling my kids, working at church (she was on staff), volunteering at school, and a hundred other things; I can't even figure out how I can find five minutes a day to be alone with God to pray!"

My point isn't to mention every potential reason why people don't enjoy God, just a few of the main ones I've seen. If you feel you're enjoying God at this point in your Christian life, keep up whatever you're doing! He needs to be enjoyed. He wants to be enjoyed. And because of who he is and everything he's done, he is most definitely worth enjoying.

If you recognize yourself in any of these scenarios or are honestly saying to yourself, "I'd like to enjoy God, but I just don't know how," I want to suggest a few hints that have helped me. Whereas in the chapters ahead, the "Making the Most" sections contain activities to do with your child to foster his spiritual growth, this "Making the Most" section is parent-centered and is aimed at helping you to experience and enjoy God's presence anew and to keep that enjoyment alive.

> For in him we live
> and move and have
> our being.
>
> —Acts 17:28

Once you have begun to enjoy God again, you can start passing this enjoyment along by helping your children look through the Wonder Window. And you won't be as likely to extinguish your kids' natural enjoyment of God, since they have a great capacity for this already.

While we'll look at ways to stir up wonder in your kids in the next chapter, remember that the Enjoying God Window starts and ends with the parent. If you enjoy God, you won't need to teach your kids to enjoy him. They'll pick it up. Enjoying God will be part of the normal Christian life.

It works like this: if parents are enjoying the wonderful blessings not only of God's banquet table but also of being with the Host, our kids will likely want to come to the table as well and partake of his blessings. There they will "taste and see that the Lord is good" and desire to receive his love and know him more. So before you continue reading, say a prayer that you will so live before your children that they'll not just walk but run to God's banquet table to join you!

Making the Most of the Enjoying God Window

Read through the Gospels in an Easy-to-Read Version or a Paraphrase of the Bible

I find that when I lose my enjoyment of God, it's usually because I've gotten hung up in the brush strokes of living the Christian life and I've lost the portrait of the Life of Christ. We continually need fresh glimpses of our Savior!

When this happens, I put down my latest novel and start reading in long stretches about Jesus. I try to picture every scene like it's a movie. I soak in his words, the nuances of how he treated people, and his miracles. I imagine myself there with him in the crowd when he fed the multitudes or visited Mary and Martha in their home in Bethany (and it's easy for me to picture myself as Martha because, like her, I'm busy and distracted about many things). I read about the last week of his life and think, *I'm the only one he did this for.* I let his pain and suffering and his broken heart overtake me. And when I finish, I'm mesmerized once again at the length and depth and breadth of his love for me.

Spend Time with Babies and Young Children

When my kids were little, I was energized by the way they looked at the world with wonder and delight. Everything was fun— lighting a fire in the fireplace on cold winter nights, lying on their backs in the grass and telling what they thought the cloud shapes looked like. Everything was exciting and new.

And each Sunday morning as I lead the kids in our prayer class at church (or as often happens, they lead *me*), I am struck by their childlike faith as they pray for Andrew's infected tooth to be healed or for God to help Abi's mom to be able to get pregnant.

Kids enjoy God much easier than we adults do! They are freer in worship and singing, quicker to confess their sins and wrongs, and more openhearted as well. Maybe that's why Jesus said, "Let the little children come to me! Never send them away! For the Kingdom of God belongs to men who have hearts as trusting as these little children's. And anyone who doesn't have their kind of faith will never get within the Kingdom's gates" (Luke 18:16–17 LB). Hanging out with kids will help restore your enjoyment of God.

Walk in Nature and Get Lost in the Details

Recently my husband, Holmes, and I were on the coast of Maine for a few days of R and R. As we sat on the huge granite rocks on Georgetown Point and watched the sun rise and the gleams of light bounce off the water and fill the whole scene with light, my heart was refreshed. Enjoying God wasn't a chore; it was a natural response to the beauty all around us.

Whether it's a rose garden in the spring, a sunset any day of the week, or a moonlit sky studded with stars, get out of your four walls, get away from the constant noise of TV, stereo, computer, call waiting, and cell phones and enjoy God in nature. He made it for us to enjoy, and he's glad when his handiwork causes our hearts to leap with joy!

Read Books That Testify to the Fact That God Is Still Doing Miracles Today

My life—like your life—sometimes feels like a testimony to the mundane. Life is life, and sometimes we feel like we're plodding through mud. Other times it's either boring or flat-out difficult. But while God is in between miracles in your life, he's very active in the lives of others. He's snatching thousands from the fires of hell on a daily basis. He's healing the sick and broken-hearted. He's answering the prayers of those who trust in him.

Reading a magazine, such as *Guideposts,* that contains testimonies of real people or a book, like Mike Yorkey's *Touched by the Savior* (Word), that tells how God came into the lives of famous and ordinary people is extremely uplifting. And reading a biography like *Coming Clean*

Bookbag

Resources for Parents

Blackaby, Henry. *Experiencing God.* Nashville: Broadman and Holman, 1993.

Campbell. Ross. *Relational Parenting.* Chicago: Moody Press, 2000.

Cymbala, Jim. *Fresh Wind, Fresh Fire.* Grand Rapids: Zondervan, 1998.

_____. *Fresh Faith: What Happens When Real Faith Ignites God's People.* Grand Rapids: Zondervan, 1999.

Piper, John. *Desiring God.* Sisters, Ore.: Multnomah, 1986.

Wilkinson, Bruce. *Experiencing Spiritual Breakthroughs: The Powerful Principle of the Three Chairs.* Sisters, Ore.: Multnomah, 1999.

(Waterbrook)—the story of Jorge Valdes and how he became a Christian after years of smuggling drugs for the Medellin Cartel—shows me that if God can be persistent and not give up on a man like this, then he will never give up on me.

Much of the church has let testimony time fall by the wayside. Yet it's an important part of realizing that God is in action all around us. And that he's still in the business of changing lives and performing signs and wonders in the hearts of people. He's bringing revival in remote villages where people have existed in darkness for centuries. If you're not consistently hearing about God's work in the world, it becomes very easy to lose the wonder of him and less easy to enjoy him on a daily basis.

Find Your Own Spiritual Pathway

Each of us, being uniquely and wonderfully made, connects with God in different ways. Maybe you don't experience God as much when reading the Bible as you do when you're jogging. Perhaps a rose garden bores you, but Handel's *Messiah* causes your spirit to soar and helps you connect with your Creator. Do you enjoy God most in corporate worship at your church, alone in the woods, or in your prayer closet? Do you like to connect with God in the early morning before the sun is up or late at night, while you're driving to work or while having devotions with your kids? Understanding your own spiritual pathway—how you best connect with God—is an important step in enjoying your relationship with him. Don't feel guilty if your way of connecting with God is different from that of your spouse or friends—just draw near to God and he promises to draw near to you (see James 4:8).

Listen to God's Voice

Nothing revitalizes your spiritual life like hearing from God. When you hear his particular heart-to-heart message meant for you, something changes. Your attitude can be transformed. A relationship can be restored or you can receive much-needed direction for your career or your parenting. Sometimes God's whispers are intended to reassure you of his love or to deliver his peace in the midst of a trying time. At other times, he may tell you of someone you should offer help to or pray for.

I've found God doesn't waste words. He is not long-winded! The Lord can literally change your life with only a few words. Ask God to speak to you and to open your "spiritual ears." Then pay attention when he taps you on the shoulder in the middle of your workday or drive time, when you're with your children or taking a walk. As you listen and respond to God's voice, you'll enjoy him in new ways.

Early childhood develops under the sign of wonder;
for the child everything is a source of wonder
because everything is new.

—Sofia Cavalletti,
The Religious Potential of the Child

To be an agent of healthy nurture is to stay
attuned to the natural wonder of a child's
discovery and enthusiasm for all of life—
to encourage emotional sensitivity and
expression, not to discourage or stifle it.

—John and Paula Sandford,
Waking the Slumbering Spirit

Wonder, amazement, awe—such are the
characteristic signatures of childhood.
Children, novice to their ever-changing world,
are alert, aware and alive to the natural
bounty constantly being revealed.

—Miriam Huffman Rockness,
A Time to Play: On Childhood and Creativity

three

the wonder window

We stood out on the lawn of a college campus waiting for the fireworks display on the Fourth of July last year. My husband, Holmes, held Caitlin, our sixteen-month-old granddaughter. Since she'd never been to a fireworks show, she couldn't imagine why we were waiting there in the heat of the summer evening. It had been a long hour-and-a-half wait, strolling her around, following as she toddled over to the kids near us, and trying to entertain her in the back of the station wagon when she got flustered and bored. We knew what was ahead, so we tried to keep this active little one busy until the light show started.

Suddenly, a huge Roman candle flew up and burst into colors of green, blue, and red on the dark canvas of the night sky. As Holmes held her, Caitlin looked up, astonished. In her eyes, I could see the colors flashing, the fireworks sparkling, and her imagination dancing. And until the last fireworks danced in the sky, that look of pure wonder lit up her expression. Even as we drove home and a weary baby fell asleep in her car seat, Caitlin's smile continued to warm our hearts.

I've seen that look of wonder when she swung in the backyard tree and glimpsed a bluebird flying overhead, when she felt the rain dripping on her head, and when she played with a simple doodlebug. "Nandy, look at this! Papa, come see! Listen to the cricket sing!" she exclaims frequently.

Children just naturally experience wonder. They wonder about why the grass is green instead of purple, why we don't have wheels

instead of feet, why God made birds that can fly but we cannot—
"Why, why, why?"

Why are so many of us grown-ups wonder-impaired?

Somehow as we get further from the wonder years of childhood, we experience less awe about much of anything—God,
nature, or everyday miracles like a baby's smile or the new sunrise
that lights up our earth morning by morning. Yet Psalm 98:1 says,
"Sing to GOD a brand-new song. He's made a world of wonders!"
(MESSAGE). Wonder is characteristic of children, poets, and artists,
and it's only possible in a person who stops
and looks, whose mind is able to "settle
and rest in things." Wonder "attracts us
with irresistible force toward the object of
our astonishment."[1]

Wonder ... a sense of surprise or state of
amazed admiration.

Wonder ... experiencing something far
beyond anything previously known.[2]

Wonder must have been what the
Israelites felt when Moses stretched out his
staff over the Red Sea and the huge waters
parted, rolling back to cut a path for them
to walk through to safety; what David the
shepherd boy felt when he slung rocks at
Goliath the giant and he keeled over dead;
what the astonished onlookers must have
felt when Lazarus walked out of the tomb at Jesus' command,
although he'd been dead several days; or what the disciples experienced when they looked around and saw that the satisfied crowd of
five thousand had miraculously been fed with only a few loaves of
bread and a few fish. Jesus had a way of inspiring awe wherever he
went.

> You are worthy, our
> Lord and God, to
> receive glory and honor
> and power, for you
> created all things, and
> by your will they were
> created and have
> their being.
>
> —REVELATION 4:11

But what about today? Does God still do things that can inspire
kids and even us? One of the first places children experience wonder and experience God is in nature. And sometimes it's the sim-
plest things that make a big impact.

Eva, a mom I know, grew up in her family's large greenhouse and nursery. She and her siblings were surrounded by thousands of varieties of plants on four acres in the middle of a large city. While there was always lots of work for the kids to do, there was a lot of fun and adventure too: playing hide-and-go-seek in the junglelike botanical garden, making secret hideouts among the trees, creating potions and experiments from flowers, berries, and leaves.

Eva's parents spread their knowledge of plants and their love for God's creation to all their customers and to the community, and they didn't leave out their children. Eva remembers her dad working with the plants in the family nursery. She'd be playing nearby, and he'd call her over to look at some new variety of plant or an unusual flower. His excitement was contagious. "How can anyone not believe in God when they look at the awesome design of this flower? This didn't happen by accident. Look at these intricate parts. They all serve a purpose; they are part of God's design."

> For by him all things were created: things in heaven and on earth, visible and invisible, whether thrones or powers or rulers or authorities; all things were created by him and for him.
>
> —Colossians 1:16

Eva isn't in the plant business as her parents were, but because of her father's enthusiasm, gentle explanations, and questions, she will always be aware of God's wonderful gifts to us in nature and is passing on the same enthusiasm for and sensitivity to God's creation to her children.

You don't have to live on a plant nursery, however, to introduce your child to the wonder of God's world. Through helping her become attentive to the five senses, you can introduce your child to the wonders of the environment, both indoors and outdoors. And you don't have to approach your child with nature as if you were a science teacher, either.

When Rachel Carson, author of *A Sense of Wonder,* tramped through the Maine woods with her young nephew Roger, she didn't make a conscious effort to identify the plants and animals by species but simply expressed her pleasure at their discoveries and called his attention to whatever caught her eye—new smells, things to touch and explore. They went nature walking "in the spirit of two friends on an expedition of exciting discovery."[3] By sharing this approach to nature, she planted seeds of wonder that impacted her nephew's life by growing into a love of nature and an observant eye. When you observe things with your child, Carson advises asking, "What if I'd never seen (or touched, heard, felt ...) this before?" and "What if I knew I would never experience it again?"[4] With this attitude, you may begin to experience wonder.

Sensational Ways to Stir Up Wonder

Parents and grandparents are essential in initiating children into lives of exploration and discovery. For children to keep their wonder alive, what is most needed, Carson says, is "the companionship of at least one adult to share in their explorations, rediscovering with them the joy, excitement, and mystery of the world."[5]

Using the five senses and whatever environment you live in, you can take your child by the hand and help her to experience the wonder of the world around her.

What if God created the world all gray? What if everything was unscented? Instead, he has made us sensual beings, says Terry Willits. "In his goodness and creativity, he has given us eyes to see, ears to hear, noses to smell, mouths to taste and talk, and bodies to feel. Each sense is a rich blessing that enhances our life in a unique way and can bring immense pleasure or pain. . . . Our senses are the way we experience life."[6] Try the following five sense activities, ways to enjoy the variety of tastes, feelings, sights, and sounds, both indoors and outdoors.

Experiencing Wonder through Touch

Holding your baby up to a tree to touch the leaves blowing in the wind or to feel the rough bark not only is stimulating but helps her grow more observant. Hold up your young child's hand to touch Grandma's face and to feel Grandpa's rough eyebrows, to trace the outline of his ear, to feel his hair (and compare it to how her own hair feels). The variety of animal furs is another touching delight. Go to a petting zoo, and as your child feels the llama's coat, the pig's hide, the turtle's shell, the donkey's or pony's mane, talk about how God made each animal and gave it just the right kind of fur or skin to protect it.

Get a brown paper bag and put objects of different textures inside (like a feather, a snakeskin, a soft cotton ball, a smooth rock). Let your child put her hand in the bag and try to guess what the item is. Also, take time to enjoy serendipitous moments to touch snowflakes falling on your face, the cool wet grass in the morning, or slimy seaweed at the beach.

> Let this be written for a future generation, that a people not yet created may praise the LORD.
>
> —PSALM 102:18

Smelling Wonders

"Smell is a potent wizard that transports us across thousands of miles and all the years we have lived," said Helen Keller. Children are often more sensitive to smells than adults, so you can easily plant seeds of wonder in your child's heart through his sense of smell.

You can start by pointing out that our capacity to sniff, smell, and enjoy a great variety of odors is one of God's wonderful gifts to us. Then you can take a "smelly walk" around the block, sniffing as you go and talking about fragrances and smells you encounter: charcoal grilling aromas or smoke from fireplaces, freshly cut grass, sweet smelling honeysuckle vines.

"God has given us so many smells to enjoy and noses to sniff with," you might say to your child. Then offer a new aroma. Your enjoyment of the wonders of smell will encourage your child to notice and be more aware of them. Sit on the front porch and smell the air after a rainstorm. Visit a community garden and point out the difference in how a rose, gardenia, or lavender smells. Let your child help you make a spicy holiday mixture with cloves, cinnamon sticks, and citrus rings. Add the mixture to some water and simmer on the stove to fill your home with a festive smell.

Visual Wonders

Whether you live in the high desert of Oregon or in a quiet valley, in a city or in a suburb, there are things around you to delight your eyes and to stir up wonder in your child: a night sky filled with stars, a glorious sunrise or sunset, a double rainbow after a storm, snowflakes falling from the sky.

One year while vacationing in Colorado, a couple we know wanted to share with their daughters Ashlyn, four, and Emma, one, the beauty of seeing God's creation. Sitting in a meadow of wildflowers by a lake, Angie and Ian asked the girls to look around them and name all the colors they could see in God's world—blue, yellow, green, red, purple, orange. Then they used those colors to make tie-dyed shirts for the family. A year later, whenever Ashlyn wears her brightly colored T-shirt, she talks about the wonderful variety of colors and flowers they saw in that Colorado meadow and how great a painter God must be to do such splendid artwork.

> For you created my inmost being; you knit me together in my mother's womb.
>
> —Psalm 139:13

Try taking a "color walk" around the block and let your kids point out all the colors they see. Or take them on a walk through your yard and garden each season to observe the different plants and bushes that bloom in each part of the year. Call them to the window to watch a rainstorm or the full moon.

Sometimes we can gently point kids to God when we notice something special, and it doesn't have to be on a mountain or in a meadow. It can even be on our back porch if we're willing to take the time. One morning while my friend Carol was having her quiet time, she saw a spider web by her back door. Dew hung on the web, and it was the most exquisite thing she'd ever seen. She set her Bible aside to seize the moment and called her girls over to show them what she'd discovered.

"Look how the web looks like thousands of sparkly diamonds!" Carol exclaimed. The girls' eyes widened as they looked at the intricacy of the spider's work.

"See what God's done? Isn't it amazing how he did that?" she added, pointing the girls to their heavenly Father. This led to a spontaneous conversation about how God had created even this spider. Carol doesn't often stand in awe of spiders, but that morning she was aware of the wonders right under her nose.

Little things we can see also stir up wonder. Stop and watch an earthworm on a driveway puddle after the rain. Get a small magnifying glass and take your child to a city rose garden or your own backyard garden. Instead of rushing through and only glancing at the blossoms, get close enough with the magnifying glass to look inside the flowers. Or take a toilet paper tube (decorate it with stickers or paint if you want to dress it up) and say, "Let's go out today and look at the grass." Your kids may likely answer, "What do you mean? We've seen grass before!" But once they are on their hands and knees with their tubes, you'll likely be pulled in several directions. One child finds a hole, and in that hole is a worm or insect. Another sees tiny flowers or spiders she never knew existed. The little things God created hold a wonder all their own.

> For we are God's workmanship, created in Christ Jesus to do good works, which God prepared in advance for us to do.
>
> —EPHESIANS 2:10

Hearing Wonders

Kids tend to hear sounds we adults miss, so they may be the ones who lead you in this sense. Caitlin, our granddaughter, perks her ears up when she hears a siren, a cat meowing next door, a squirrel scurrying across the leaf-covered yard.

Take time to notice the sound of blowing leaves in the wind, the crackling sound the leaves make in the late autumn before they fall from their limbs and drift to the ground, the distinct song of the bobwhite, the chatter of blue jays or woodpeckers in your back yard. Turn off the radio and television when it rains and listen to the raindrops tapping on the roof. In the summertime, listen to the sound of the crickets and locusts. If you listen closely, you can even show your children how to tell the temperature by counting the number of cricket chirps in fifteen seconds and multiplying by eight.

A Taste of Wonder

A taste of wonder may be the most fun of all for kids: the taste of cool water on a hot day, a juicy watermelon or crisp apple, the taste of hot cocoa or smooth chocolate. To help your child experience the contrast and variety of tastes, put something bitter, sour, sweet, and salty in little bowls. Then blindfold him and let him guess what the foods are.

We can experience wonder at daily mealtimes if we take time to savor and enjoy the variety of foods God has provided us to enjoy— even a simple banana.

Ryan sat in his booster chair and began peeling his banana.

"You know, Ryan," his mother, Ellen, called from the sink. "God grew that banana just for you." The preschooler gave his mom a quizzical look and took a bite. "No other boy in the entire world will ever get to see the inside of that particular piece of fruit."

Instead of gobbling it down like he usually did, Ryan eyed the banana thoughtfully before taking another bite.

"Every shiny cell was formed for you to enjoy. Every yummy bite and sweet scent was created by your heavenly Father, because he created everything!" As Ryan finished his banana and threw the peel away, she added, "There will be no other banana just like yours, and there will be no other boy just like you."

Did Ellen get a big response from her four-year-old? Not hardly. But it's part of the "wonder puzzle" that is imparted over time. I can almost guarantee you won't get an immediate response from your child, but it's not the immediate you're after. It's the eternal. And developing eternal responses and building an attitude of wonder take time.

> But now, this is what the LORD says—he who created you, O Jacob, he who formed you, O Israel: "Fear not, for I have redeemed you; I have summoned you by name; you are mine."
>
> —ISAIAH 43:1

Your goal is to plant an extraordinary seed in her mind that, with cultivation, will sprout when you least expect it.

Wired for Wonder

From a young age to the time they leave home, you can impart and share wonder with your child. Naturally, it's best to begin when they're young. To sit with a child and watch his eyes get big at new discoveries builds a sense of awe into a young heart. And as the years go by and you continue to point out the wonder of God, it confirms what you've already built and helps to renew your own sense of wonder as well.

And it's not just through sunsets, flowers, or uplifting praise music that we can point our children to God. While a magnificent Bach organ piece can cause my friend Peggy to go into the third heaven and my friend Connie can see glimpses of God in singing birds and the aspen trees in Colorado, there are so many more things that point to God. Every person is wired differently in how they discover, relate to, and enjoy God.

If your son is computer-oriented and fascinated with physics, you can point out that God created logic and the principles that make computers, math, and physics work. When your ten-year-old gets excited about Gila monsters and other exotic lizards (that you are grossed out by), you can say, "Look, that's about God! He created it just for you to enjoy" (and then point out the practical purpose that lizards serve in nature). If your daughter loves people, you can share how creative God is in making all the colors, languages, races, and unique kinds of people in the world. Whatever little or big things excite your child's heart, they can be glimpses of the wonder and majesty and creativity of God.

Remember, however, to make time and space for wonder. In a culture moving in fast-forward, it's easy to overschedule our children's every waking minute so there's no time for observing things, questioning, or exploring. Sofia Cavalletti offered wise counsel for parents and teachers on this issue. Avoid giving kids too many things and offering too many stimuli too fast. "If the child does not have the time to dwell on anything, then everything will come to seem the same to him and he will lose all interest in things," she says.[7] Giving your child the gift of time will be a lifelong blessing!

Making the Most of the Wonder Window

In this section are ideas about how to build wonder and enjoyment in your child's life, from the earliest years and beyond, or to stir up that wonder if it has faded.

Search the Skies
(Ages 4 and up)

Be as amazed as David the shepherd boy was when he looked up into the night sky to see a zillion stars. If you live where city lights dim the stellar wonder, plan an evening out to a park or football field or drive to the country. Check out some books on stargazing at your library. Can you identify the constellations? Can you count those twinkling stars? Any planets in sight? Share with your kids what comes to mind when you look up into the sky. Tell them how you feel when you realize that the same Maker of the galaxies crafted each one of you, knows all about you, and wants to have a deep relationship with you.

Journal Jots

For Your Child to Write About

• What one lesson have you learned by exploring God's creation? Why is it so special?
• Write Bible verses that come to mind that talk about the amazing world God made. See the Scripture verses quoted throughout this chapter to get you started.

Quality and Quantity
(Ages 6 and up)

• Get a book from your local library on sketching people.
• Go to a place you can observe people (a park, store, or mall).
• Choose what body part (nose, eye, mouth, ear, legs) you'd like to observe that day.

- Observe the variety of shapes and sizes of that body part on different people. Sketch the variety of shapes and sizes you see. Doesn't God love variety?

Pretty Fishy
(Ages 5 and up)

- Check out a book on creatures of the deep, then visit an aquarium or lake and identify the kinds of fish there. Draw a picture of your favorite fish.
- Discover the ways that people explore the underwater sea world. Journal your finds.
- Which stories from the Bible make reference to fish? Jonah and the whale, Christ multiplying the fish for the crowds, Peter finding money in the fish's mouth. How many types of fish are mentioned in Scripture?

Spontaneous Stop
(Ages 2 and up)

- When you see geese making a V-line south, drop what you're doing and call your kids to the window. Mimic the noises they make. How many geese do you see?
- Find the new season's "firsts": spring firsts

Bookworm

Resources for Children

Ganeri, Anita. *The Ocean Atlas.* New York: Dorling Kindersley, 1994. For all ages.

Lambier, Doug, and Robert Stevenson. *Genesis for Kids: Science Experiments That Show God's Power in Creation!* Nashville: Nelson, 1997. For ages 8–14.

Seymour, Simon. *Comets, Meteors and Asteroids.* New York: William Morrow, 1998. For ages 4 up.

_____. *Our Solar System.* New York: William Morrow, 1992. For ages 5 up.

Showers, Paul and Kay Showers. *Before You Were a Baby.* New York: HarperCollins, 1968. For ages 5–9.

Sweetland, Nancy. *God's Quiet Things.* Grand Rapids: Eerdmans, 1994. For ages 4–8.

(crocus to bloom, tree to bud), summer firsts (90 degree day, day to swim), autumn firsts (pumpkin on the vine, tree with leaves changing colors), winter firsts (frost, snowman, sledding day).

- Point out the brilliant colors in a sunrise or sunset. Pause together for a moment to enjoy the everyday wonders God lavishes around you.

Heart to Heart

Think It Over and Share with Your Child

- Think about what each of your children is most interested in or fascinated by, because whatever it is can be a key to their hearts and a window through which they can relate to God. Whether it's music, art, computers, science, sports, weather, animals, or a myriad of other interests, bring God into it—because he made it all!
- Describe to your children what reminds you of God's power.
- What catastrophic experience, like watching a tornado pick up a house or water flood the street, has helped you understand God as Creator? God means what he

says about being thankful "in all things." Your children will learn thankfulness by your example.

- Go ahead. Push aside paying the bills or washing the lunch dishes for five minutes and enjoy God's creation. Tell a favorite story or read a poem that talks of people and/or nature.
- Remember that variety of color, shapes of snowflakes, sizes of animals, and personalities of people are all part of God's handiwork. Point out these awesome traits, saying, "Hey, look at what God did! Isn't that incredible? What a creative God we serve!"

Lots of Languages
(Ages 6 and up)

Even at the Tower of Babel God manifested his affluent way of creating variety.

- Discover how many language groups there are.
- Check out a foreign language study program on cassette.
- Compare a foreign language to the English language. How many characters does it have? Are the characters the same or different from those in English? Are they similar in sound? How is the sentence structured; for example, article, subject, verb, indirect object, direct object?
- Invite an international student from a local university to your home for a meal. Ask him to speak in his native language and to teach you and your children a few words.

Wayfaring Stranger
(Ages 5 and up)

Experience other cultures in your "own back yard." Choose a country to "visit." Find a well-illustrated book that details the country's culture, including form of government, traditions, primary language, and history. (The

Bookbag

Resources for Parents

Golden Guide series. New York: Golden Press. Includes topics on trees, weather, insects, etc.

Morris, Neil. *What Is My Shadow Made Of? Questions Kids Ask about Everyday Science.* Pleasantville, N.Y.: Reader's Digest, 1995. For ages 6 and up.

Nappa, Mike and Amy. *Imagine That! 365 Wacky Ways to Build a Creative Christian Family.* Minneapolis: Augsburg/Fortress, 1998.

Quinn, Mary C., Rachel Fisher, and Barbara S. Garriel. *12 Take-Home Thematic Backpacks.* New York: Professional, 1994. For ages 5–9.

Roberts, Janet Wier, and Carole Huelbig. *City Kids and City Critters.* New York: McGraw-Hill, 1996. For ages 5–12.

internet may have helpful information.) Find a cookbook that gives recipes of your chosen country's traditional foods and prepare a course or an entire meal.

Baby Bundles
(Ages 6 and up)

- Visit the maternity ward to watch the newborns. Which babies have hair? Compare features such as nose shapes and eyes squints. Listen to the babies' cries.
- Volunteer to work in the church nursery. Afterward, discuss the babies and their unique personalities, appearances, and other traits.

Zoo Sleuth
(Ages 2 and up)

Hand out a checklist of animals and objects to be discovered next time you and your kids visit the zoo. Ask some questions that will spur interest. Talk about God's incredible creativity in making all the different animals. Here are some examples:

Zoo Clues (Answers are in italics.)

1. Where is the kiwi's native home? *New Zealand*
   Can it fly? *No*
   What does it eat? *Nocturnal kiwis eat worms*
2. What does a platypus look like? *It has webbed feet and a bill like a duck*
   What do the females feed their young? *Milk; it's a mammal*
3. What sizes do stingrays come in? *From a width of 5 inches to 7 feet*
4. How many marsupials (pouched mammals) can you find? *Kangaroo, opossum, wombat, koala, etc.*
5. Where does the yak live? *The Himalayan Mountains*
6. How do starfish reproduce? *They lay eggs*
   How many eggs do female starfish produce in one year? *200 million*

Stash the Trash
(Ages 3 and up)

Take care of the world God gave us. Here's how.

- Collect trash as you take a walk in the park or down your street. Notice God's creatures (birds, squirrels, etc.) and talk about the ill effects improper waste disposal has on them (plastic gets caught around an animal's neck, diseases spread).

- Gather information on organizations that help keep our world clean and safe. (Use discretion. God gave us "rule over every living thing" as much as he gave us the responsibility to maintain it. "Saving the [you fill in the blank]" can get a little out of hand. Watch that you do not become too focused on the creation rather than the Creator.)

Worship is the hallmark of the truly Christian home. What do I mean by worship in a very practical day-to-day reality? I mean an exalting of who God is and who He desires to be in relationship with us, a recognition by all members of the family that our lives come from and are ruled by God.

—Phil Phillips,
Helping Your Children Walk with God

God is at work in the lives of our children as they learn and in us as we teach and nurture them.

—Dorothy B. Fritz,
The Child and the Christian Faith

The worship most acceptable to God comes from a thankful and cheerful heart.

—Plutarch

four

the **worship** window

Wonder is a marvelous thing; to lose it is to lose one of the most lovely things in life. But wonder alone isn't enough. Wonder was experienced by the pagans, who were so in awe of the sun, moon, and stars, that they made gods out of them and worshiped at altars of their own making. As Ravi Zacharias writes, "In childhood years, wonder can be attained by dabbling in the world of fantasy. That is both the glory and the fragility of childhood. But as the years pass, wonder is eroded in the face of reality and in the recognition that life may not be lived in a fairy-tale world. A displacement is brought about by the ever-increasing demand of the mind, not just for the fantastic, but for the truth."[1]

And Sofia Cavalletti writes that "it is in this quest for truth where we must meet each child we're entrusted with and help point them to the Source of every good and every perfect gift. Because without a worthy object, wonder will be quenched. Finite, limited objects will inevitably disappoint children."[2]

That's where worship comes in, where we help our children connect with God, learn about his character, develop an attitude of gratitude toward his marvelous acts, and develop a positive view of life and of themselves as created by God. As Scripture says, we must speak of the truth to our children and nurture this truth as we walk them to the park, get them ready for school, or tuck them in for a bedtime story.

Responding to God with Gratitude

Wonder, as we saw in the last chapter, is our awe-filled response, our "wow!" to creation, and with a little pointing in the right direction, it can lead us and our children to worship. Long ago, David said, "Many, O LORD my God, are the wonders you have done" (Ps. 40:5); "The heavens declare the glory of God; the skies proclaim the work of his hands" (Ps. 19:1).

When he looked at what God had made in the heavens and on the earth, the psalmist acknowledged God's hand in creation; the wonders he saw led him to proclaim the goodness of God. In worship we experience and respond to God, giving him credit for what he's done, praising him, and thanking him. Kids are good at the wonder part. It's only a few steps from wonder to worship, and within that process comes a deep enjoyment of God. How does it happen? It first begins with realizing that we're being watched by our children, so our example and our spiritual lives are of the utmost importance. We must embrace the privilege God has given us of guiding them. It also begins with an invitation, in a sense—welcoming our kids to the God we love and worship.

> Let everything that has breath praise the LORD. Praise the LORD.
>
> —PSALM 150:6

Karen, a mother of two daughters, says, "When I enjoy God myself and make that enjoyment an everyday part of life, when I share my gratefulness to him, I'm helping my children learn to enjoy God by being thankful for his creation." Karen shares her appreciation of a flower, a butterfly, or a beautiful sunset with her children. One day they tried to come up with words to describe how leaves sound when the wind blows them along the street. As they did, Karen shared with Christine and Katherine, "I'm so thankful God made autumn. I'm so glad he made these golden and red leaves! Isn't it an interesting sound when they blow around in the wind?"

When the girls were two and three years old, Karen and her daughters ran down to the end of the street so they could see a beautiful double rainbow. Years later, the girls still remember that day. As Karen naturally shared those "God moments" when she saw God working in their lives, she gave credit where credit was due. When God worked something out for the best or placed something beautiful in their path, she acknowledged his hand instead of chalking it up to serendipity. Then she began to see her girls attributing good things to God. When they make it across a big street safely (an accomplishment since Karen and one of the girls are visually impaired), Christine will say, "Thank you, God, for getting us across safely." When she does well on a test, she says, "Thank you, Lord, I couldn't have done it without you!"

Our joy in God can be contagious. Patty loves praise music and often plays it while she does housework. When her two boys were babies, she would scoop them up in her arms and dance with them whenever she heard a certain praise song. As they grew and became mobile, they would wiggle out of her arms and dance around her as she danced. Holding hands, twirling, and singing, mother and sons experienced God's joy until the song was over and then, exhausted, collapsed on the floor in giggles. As time wore on, the kids picked up the habit and called her when they heard something wonderful on the radio, wanting to drop everything and dance as she'd taught them. The boys are now eight and eleven, but they still love to connect with and worship God through movement.

I praise you because I am fearfully and wonderfully made; your works are wonderful, I know that full well. My frame was not hidden from you when I was made in the secret place. When I was woven together in the depths of the earth, your eyes saw my unformed body. All the days ordained for me were written in your book before one of them came to be.

—PSALM 139:14–16

Knowing God's Character

"Men will trust in God no further than they know Him," said Jonathan Edwards. Psalm 9:10 affirms that truth: "Those who know your name will trust in you." An important dimension of worship is learning about God's character and acknowledging or praising him for who he is—what the Psalms call "blessing his name." This is the element in worship we call praise, and it doesn't have to be a complicated process.

In an attempt to teach her four-year-old son, David, about the names of God, Lori explained that "Abba, Father" means "Daddy" and encouraged him to talk to God as if talking to his best friend or, even better, his own daddy. When David was tempted to pray the same thing each night, she suggested he ask God, "What's the best thing that happened to you today, God?" because at dinnertime, that's the question they ask each family member to share about their day, including Dad.

The family had a new puppy at the time, and Lori was growing weary of caring for it. It was taking more of her time than she'd expected; they'd planned for the puppy to be the kids' responsibility.

So a few days later, when Lori was putting David to bed and praying with him, the boy asked his new question, "God, what's the best thing that happened to you today?" They waited a few brief moments for the reply, and Lori asked, "David, what did God say?"

"Hmmm," he hesitated. "I think God said the best thing was that I took the puppy out for his business and fed and watered him so Mommy wouldn't have to. He was happy about that!"

Carol, a homeschool mom, took just a few moments with her girls each morning, before beginning their academic work, to look at some verses in the Psalms and have them write down all the names of God or characteristics of God they could find in those verses. It became a kind of treasure hunt. They looked for God; they recorded what they found. Then at night as they prayed, Carol led them in praising God specifically for the attributes they'd discovered that day. As the girls added a few names and characteristics each week, along with the Scripture references for each, they got to know the character of God better and better. And they found they would never run out of reasons to praise God.

Entering His Courts with Praise

Baby Zach lay quietly as his grandma sang, "Praise the name of Jesus; Praise the name of Jesus." He cooed and voluntarily lifted his arms in worship. This wasn't an unusual gesture for Zach. His mom and dad often sang songs of praise to God, lifting up their hands while holding him on their laps. He had witnessed his parents worshiping, and at ten months, he too praised God with lifted hands.

As people filled the streets of Jerusalem during Jesus' triumphant entry, the children excitedly waved palm branches and joined in praising and worshiping him. When we praise God, we are powerful examples for our children. Earl and Peggy, parents of five kids, love to praise God in song and prayer. So over the years, the children have had many opportunities to come into God's presence during family worship times—singing praise songs, sharing from the Word, and praying. Earl and Peggy found that when Dad came into God's presence as he played his guitar and sang, the children would follow—not every time, but often. And even now that they're grown, when they come home for a visit, they look forward to family worship time.

> Shout for joy to the LORD, all the earth. Worship the LORD with gladness; come before him with joyful songs. Enter his gates with thanksgiving and his courts with praise; give thanks to him and praise his name.
>
> —PSALM 100:1-2, 4

Wonderfully Made

When their children were very young, Tom and Brenda very intentionally taught them to praise God through Psalm 139, the "fearfully and wonderfully made" psalm. As the kids grew, Tom and Brenda pointed out the unique physical characteristics of each child. Birthmarks, freckles, teeth (and the loss of teeth) all became fair game for the parents to point to and say, "Isn't God creative! I'm so glad he didn't make us all alike. Wouldn't the world be a boring place if we all had the same hair color or nose shape?" All the children learned at an early age that "flaws" aren't flaws at all; they are God's handiwork.

Tom and Brenda always made a point to talk about their own features as well. "Dad's losing his hair. I bet God is happy he doesn't have to count so many anymore." Believe it or not, even stretch marks from having children can become a source of wonder and worship when the child is reminded that "Mom has them because God let us have you."

> I can do everything through him who gives me strength.
>
> —PHILIPPIANS 4:13

But in pointing out and thanking God for the wonders of diversity, Tom and Brenda didn't stop with their own family. They conveyed that every person has value to God and is fashioned in his image, that God loves the disabled child in a wheelchair just as he loves the football star or beauty queen. They didn't ignore the differences in color either. Like other unique physical characteristics, the color of someone's skin was a true gift that the Giver needed to be praised for. As a result, their children grew up with a deep sense of gratitude for how God had created them and a deep respect and compassion for others.

Children in Worship

One of the best programs I know of—used in churches around the world—to bring young children into God's presence in worship is called Children in Worship. In our discussion of the Worship Window, we can't leave out this marvelous approach to helping kids experience God. Developmentally appropriate for three- to six-year-olds, Children in Worship helps children experience God while learning about him.[3]

In this program, children experience the fourfold order of worship: assemble in God's name (call to worship, songs of praise, greeting), proclaim God's Word (through Scripture and sermon), give thanks to God (the Lord's Prayer, the Lord's Supper or Eucharist, the prayer of thanksgiving), and go in God's name (hymn, charge, blessing)—on a simple yet profound level. Through their experience in the children's worship center, the children come to understand the symbols and actions of the adult worship service. The program leader uses a sensorimotor style of storytelling and signing to relate stories of God, and most important, children have an opportunity to encounter God for themselves.

> From the lips of children
> and infants you have
> ordained praise because
> of your enemies,
> to silence the foe
> and the avenger.
>
> —PSALM 8:2

Using wooden figures such as sheep, a shepherd, and other Bible characters (which are wrapped in gold gift packages to symbolize the surprise and mystery contained within Bible Stories), children reenact parables. To encourage the child's thinking, the storyteller asks "I wonder" questions such as "I wonder how the Good Shepherd feels about his sheep" and "I wonder if the sheep feel secure in the Shepherd's care." Children respond to the stories of God with art materials and story figures. There is no rush to finish. It is a time and space set apart for God.

During response time, some children draw; others retell the story by themselves with the wooden figures and hands-on materials. The children learn to be quiet in God's presence and find the quiet place within themselves. You have to see Children in Worship to fully understand, so I highly recommend visiting one of the worship centers where this approach is used or reading *Young Children in Worship* by Sonja M. Stewart and Jerome W. Berryman.

Getting out of the Box

As children learn to experience God, they discover they can enjoy and worship him in all kinds of places and for all kinds of reasons. They can encounter God in the corporate gathering, but they don't have to be in a church setting to feel close to him. "I feel really close to God when I ride my bike," said Chelsea, eleven. "I just spill all my thoughts out; sometimes I use tunes from songs I know and make up songs to sing to him. Or just talk. I think it's the best time of the day."

Children feel close to God at lots of different times and in all kinds of places. "When I feel lonely and have no friends, when bad things happen to me, I feel God holding me in his arms and I feel safe," said Tiffany, ten. "When I read the Bible and sing praise hymns aloud with happiness," said Adam, thirteen, and Daniel, eight, agreed.

"When I walk my puppy after Bible club at school, I enjoy God and feel close to him," said eight-year-old Christian.

"When my family went to Daddy's school and we found a cat there. I thought God provided him for me and I thanked him for this blessing!" said Linda, six.

Such children, only a few years on this earth, often seem closer to heaven and to God's heart than we are, and often *they* are the ones leading us to him. May we be sensitive to our children's hearts, realize the opportunities all around us to enjoy God, and together worship the King!

Making the Most of the Worship Window

The activities in this section are designed to help kids worship and praise God, both at home and church, and express thanks for how he's created them, their families, and the world around them.

A Service of Worship
(Ages 3 and up)

Go through the order of worship that your particular church follows and explain each part to your child. Use demonstrations, objects, art, or any method that can make abstract ideas concrete. Perhaps you could also ask your pastor if he would have a series of children's sermons or children's church sessions that will help kids realize the meaning of the different parts of the worship service, such as the call to worship, songs and hymns, prayers of confession and thanksgiving, the proclamation of God's Word through the sermon, and the benediction. Take time to praise and adore him in family worship times, using some of the elements of church worship services as well.

Windows of Meaning
(Ages 5 and up)

Rituals, symbols, and ceremonies at church, such as the Lord's Supper and baptism, plus celebrations such as Christmas, Easter, Pentecost, and others have the potential to communicate truth to children and can be a way for them to experience God if we take the time to explain. Remember that in any service, there are impressionable children in the audience who are amazed and wondering what the adults are doing. Communicate to your kids the meaning behind these worship times; they may not fully understand them, but you'll be prompting them to ponder the abundant life of Christ through these ceremonies and traditions.

A to Z Praise
(All ages)

Sometimes we spend more time praising God for what he does than for who he is. With the alphabet, the Bible, and a concordance, you can help your children to know God's character better and to worship him. Create a little book, using a different letter of the alphabet each day (or week) to make a page with several verses on a characteristic of

Heart to Heart

Think It Over and Share with Your Child

Share your hope for each child. Be specific and personal:

"Janessa, I pray that you use your violin playing to encourage others and bring God glory. He gave you a special talent."

"Karen, I asked God this morning to remind you that you can do all things through him, even to be patient while you learn algebra. And look at all the progress you've made."

God. Let your children illustrate it. Go all the way from A to Z. Here's an example:

- Start with *A*. God was *able* to deliver Daniel from the mouths of the lions and to save the three Israelite friends from the fiery furnace (Dan. 3 and 6). He is just as able to save those who come to him through Christ (Heb. 7:25). He is able to guard you (2 Tim. 1:12) and keep you from stumbling (Jude 1:24), and much more.
- For *C,* James 5:11 tells us God is *compassionate.* As a father pities his children and has compassion on them, so the Lord pities those who look to him (Ps. 103:13). He is gracious and full of compassion (Ps. 111:4). His compassion never fails; it is new every morning (Lam. 3:22–23).
- For *F,* God is *faithful.* "For the word of the LORD is right and true; he is faithful in all he does" (Ps. 33:4). "He is the faithful God, keeping his covenant of love to a thousand generations (Deut. 7:9). "The LORD is faithful to all his promises" (Ps. 145:13).
- For *G,* God is *great.* Discover God's greatness in these verses: Exodus 15:11; Deuteronomy 32:3–4; 1 Chronicles 16:25–27; and 1 Chronicles 29:10–13; Job 36:24–26; Psalms 77:12–14, 86:10, 92:5, 95:3–5, 104:1, 145:3–6; Isaiah 12:5–6.

Journal Jots

For Your Child to Write About

At the close of the day, write God a prayer of thanks. Thank him for how much he loves you, how he helped you through a problem, or how he encouraged you through your parents.

Celestial Antiphon (Ages 6 and up)

Form three groups. Read from Revelation the antiphon that takes place in heaven. (An antiphon is a verse of a psalm or hymn said or chanted in response to another.)

1. The four living creatures: "Holy, holy, holy is the

Lord God Almighty, who was, and is, and is to come" (Rev. 4:8).

2. The twenty-four elders: "You are worthy, our Lord and God, to receive glory and honor and power, for you created all things, and by your will they were created and have their being" (Rev. 4:11).

3. Voices of many angels: "Worthy is the Lamb, who was slain, to receive power and wealth and wisdom and strength and honor and glory and praise!" (Rev. 5:12). You can also use Psalm 136 for a "celestial antiphon."

Amusing Music (Ages 8 and up)

We serve a God who is worthy to be praised, and we can praise him with instruments. In 2 Samuel 6, for example, David and 30,000 Israelites played cymbals, stringed instruments, horns, and lyres and sang as they took the ark back to Jerusalem. Scripture talks about unusual instruments used in worship during Bible times. Discover what these instruments looked like and how they were made. Do any resemble a modern-day instrument?

Bookworm

Resources for Children

Bratton, Heidi. *Celebrate Family* and *Celebrate Feelings*. St. Louis: Concordia, 2000. For ages 3–6.

Bratton, Heidi, and Sally Anne Conan. *Little Ways to Give God Praise, The Little Shepherd, Where is God? Rejoice! Jesus Welcomes Me*. Mahwah, N.J.: Paulist, 1999. A series of board books for ages 0–5.

Silverstein, Shel. *The Giving Tree*. New York: HarperCollins, 1964. For ages 5 and up.

Vesey, Denise. *God Is Very Holy*. Colorado Springs: Cook Communications, 2000. For ages 4–7; includes parenting guide.

_____. *God Knows What's Best for Me*. Colorado Springs: Cook Communications, 2000. For ages 4–7; includes parenting guide.

- harp   Revelation 14:2
- cornet   Psalm 98:6
- sackbut   Daniel 3:5

Resources for Parents

Rainey, Dennis and Barbara. *Parenting Today's Adolescent*. Nashville: Nelson, 1998.

Stewart, Sonja M., and Jerome W. Berryman. *Young Children and Worship*. Louisville: Westminster/John Knox, 1989.

Hosanna to the Son of David (Ages 2 and up)

The children excitedly waved palm branches as they filled the streets of Jerusalem with praises to Jesus (see Matt. 21:9–11, 15–16). It doesn't have to be Palm Sunday to worship the Lord in this manner! During one of your family worship times, make some palm branches out of construction paper or cut small branches from a tree. Have a time of singing to the Lord (songs such as "Our God is an Awesome God," "Holy, Holy, Holy" or "Praise Him, Praise Him, All You Little Children") as you wave your "palm branches" in adoration.

Twenty Thank-Yous (All ages)

See how many thank-yous you can offer God. Go around the room as fast as you can. No two thank-yous can be alike. Begin by saying, "Thank you for ..."

- my dad, who works hard at the motor shop to buy me shoes
- my mom, who makes pancakes for my breakfast
- ears for hearing the cardinal sing
- hands for picking up my cocker spaniel, Alex

Wonderfully Made (Ages 3 and up)

Every person is "wonderfully made" by God. Discover what each child is able to do.

- How high you can jump; how fast you can run. (Check out some exercise books and learn how to stretch. Understand the anatomy of the body and what muscles are used in the exercises.)
- How long you can hold your breath.
- How fast you can read.
- How well you can sing or play an instrument.

The acceptance children receive from parents and siblings greatly influences whether they are able to thank God for how he designed them. Many kids see themselves in a negative light. A great way to encourage acceptance is to read Psalm 139 together with your child, pointing out specific things it says about how God feels about her. (God knows me and I'm precious to him. He made everything about me. His works are wonderful, so I must be wonderful. He's planned all my days, and there's nowhere I can go that he won't be with me. He knows every word before I say it! No matter where I am, God will lead me. Even though there are six billion people on the earth, this psalm says nobody is exactly like me. He understands me and has plans for me.) Then thank God for how he made your child—the color of her hair, her gifts and talents, her sense of humor.

I'm Glad You're Here!
(All ages)

In turn, recognize each family member on a day other than their birthday or another holiday.

- Make their favorite meal.
- Plant encouraging notes in places where they are sure to find them.
- Form a circle with the special person sitting in the center. Have each person say something they appreciate about that person. You may want to begin with "I'm glad you were born because ..." Be sure not to qualify the statement with "You used to get on my nerves when you ... but now ..." Or by putting yourself or someone else down, "I can't do ... as good as you." Praise them for who they are, not just for

how well they perform. "Jenny, you have a contagious laugh. Whenever I am down, I can count on your joyfulness to make me smile."

part two

loving God

Wonder comes naturally to children and can easily lead them to worship and enjoyment of God, as we've seen in the last section. They begin to understand that God created everything and "has the whole world in his hands." But how do they begin to experience a loving God? When do the familiar words to the song "Jesus Loves Me, This I Know" become not just a melody from childhood but a deep knowing, *I'm his child and he really loves me*? When does the truth of the first verse most kids memorize—John 3:16: "For God so loved the world that He gave His only begotten Son" (NKJV)—hit home and the heart open wide to receive his love?

A child can hear about God's love, sing about God's love, go to a church where the pastor eloquently preaches about God's love, and even study God's love in the Bible. But knowing and experiencing how much God deeply loves him—with an everlasting, unconditional love—is an amazing and mysterious process that starts very early in life—in fact, in infancy. And here's the scary part: it's a process that we have the greatest influence on.

What an amazing thing it is that God longs for us to open our hearts, that he wants us—and our children—"to love him because he first loved us, and yet he made us with free will so we can accept his love or reject it."[1]

In the Loving God Window, we'll look at children's longing for love and how loving God and our children with all our hearts sets the stage for our kids to begin to know God's love. When we receive God's love for *us*, we can nurture our children and tap into God's resources rather than loving them in our own strength—all with a hope that our children will experience God's love for themselves and love him back. In the Bible Window, we will see how to help our children know God and his love through his Word, since the Bible contains hundreds of declarations and descriptions of his love. In the Prayer Window, we will see prayer as a conversation between two people who love each other and how to teach our kids to dialogue with God in prayer.

God is love.

—I John 4:8

God's love for us is proclaimed with each sunrise.

—Anonymous

Every response to your child's behavior teaches her
what God is like—not because God is like you but
because her first thought about God is that God is
a person most like her parents, the persons she
knows most about.... How you treat her teaches
her what she is. Treat her as a gift of God.

—C. Sybil Waldrop,
Guiding Your Child toward God

God loves us with an everlasting love and draws us
with cords of love. That is the truth! His love is gentle
and he will never force us, but in his supreme goodness,
he desires to draw us to himself and never let us go.

—Hilary, 19

five

the loving **God** window

Part of our privilege as parents is to help introduce our children to God's love. During their infancy and childhood years, they love to be nurtured, protected, listened to, accepted, cherished, and cared for. "In early childhood the child's fundamental need is to be loved with a protective love, and to have someone to love.... It is only in love, and not in fear, that one may have a moral life worthy of the name. The older child will not be a slave who abstains from doing certain things for fear of punishment, but he will be a person who is free and empowered by love," says Sofia Cavalletti.[2]

Kids are like love-sponges. They soak up all the love parents, grandparents, aunts, or whoever is around them will offer. Open your arms, and most kids will run into them for a hug. But love isn't just something they want. They need it to thrive and to grow spiritually, emotionally, and mentally.

"Every human being longs for unfailing love. Lavish love. Focused love. Radical love. Love we can count on," writes Beth Moore.[3] Ultimately, what every person is longing for is the unfailing love of God. And as Christian parents, we want our kids to know and love God. But where do we start? It all begins by loving our children.

"The child's underlying attitude toward God (and especially his love) is primarily formed in the process of interacting with adults, especially parents.... Expressions of love, respect for the child's interest, consistent and reasonable discipline, and ethical behavior all combine to provide a positive base for a healthy God concept."[4]

If the child is loved by his parents, he is more likely to believe God loves him. He may misunderstand God later or be disappointed with hypocritical people in the church. But if the child has this solid foundation and his love tank has been filled, later "misunderstandings about God can be minimized, or at least survived."[5]

In contrast, if a child is regularly yelled at, abusively punished, and has experienced broken promises and a lack of love from his parents, it's harder to receive God's love. The truth is, kids see God's love through the filter of parental love. A mom and dad's tender, loving care of a child from infancy on lays a spiritual foundation of trust and love.

That's a huge responsibility! So how do we begin? The first step is to open your heart wider to God's love, because it's hard to give away what you don't have. God is love. And each of us was created to experience love and to enjoy a deep, loving relationship with him; yet many Christians never go there. Many of us go to church Sunday after Sunday but don't go to a relationship.

> Let us love one another, for love comes from God. Whoever loves is a child of God and knows God.
>
> —1 JOHN 4:7 tev

Ask yourself, "How do I know God loves me, not just the whole world? Have I really experienced God's love?" Maybe you're like my friend Patsy, who knew all the attributes of God, knew the correct terms for the Trinity, and could recite the Apostles' Creed by heart, but when she thought about approaching God as Father, she drew a blank. She knew God loved everybody in the world (the Bible said so) but didn't know he loved her personally.

Maybe you're a little like Jim, whose father loved him very conditionally—he seemed to care only about how his son performed, how many soccer games he won, and how many A's he made in school. He thought God loved him only when he succeeded and achieved.

Or like my friend Cyndi, who as a young Christian struggled with believing God loved her, because she came from a divorced family with a faithless, alcoholic father who could never be depended on. Once Cyndi owned up to the fact that she had difficulty experiencing God's love, a youth leader who knew her struggle encouraged her to pray every single day, "Lord, teach me that you love me."

Throughout her twenties and thirties, Cyndi continued praying that prayer each day and found herself consistently discovering how much God loved her. As a result, God's love became a real anchor in her life, even when tragedy struck and she was widowed. That's a prayer God loves to answer! And believing in his love for you is an undergirding truth that if internalized not only in your head but also in your heart, will do more than anything to enable you to help your child know and experience God's love.

> As dearly loved children … live a life of love, just as Christ loved us.
>
> —EPHESIANS 5:1–2

So whether you identify with Cyndi, Jim, or Patsy, whether you had great parents or not, asking yourself the question, "Do I know God's love for *me?*" will put you on the path to experiencing it.

Loving Your Child

Next, help your child experience love by modeling it. Make sure she knows how it feels to be loved, cherished, protected, accepted, and nurtured. Love for a child consists of adults noticing him and the things that interest him. Love for the young child is usually very physical. Cuddling and patting are important for both boys and girls. Love also needs to be verbal. Words spoken at those times when the child is being physically loved reinforce the actions. Expressions of love need to be independent of a child's behavior. Love that must be earned is far too fragile a thing for any child to depend on. For if it can be earned, it can also be lost.[6]

Part of being loved is discipline—not harsh punishment but firm, patient, loving correction. Discipline is the process of shaping your child's will, "molding attitudes and behavior in a careful and loving manner,"[7] gradually calling your child forth from foolishness to maturity. (In chapter 9 we're going to talk more about grace and loving discipline.)

None of us are going to be perfect parents. But we can make the path wider and smoother for God's love to reach our children's hearts.

If children don't experience being loved by their parents, it may be a long time before they can dismantle the view of an unloving God and begin to experience his love for them.

If you've never given your life to Christ and have never truly received his love and gift of salvation, you can simply come to God. Acknowledge that you're a sinner and can't save yourself, that only Jesus can save you; he has paid the penalty for all of your sins—past, present, and future. Give him your life and ask him to be your Savior. If you do this sincerely, God promises, "If anyone is in Christ, he is a new creation; the old has gone, the new has come!" (2 Cor. 5:17).

From Parents' Love to God's Love

Hilary, a young woman I know, shared with me how she came to know and receive the love of God and began to love him back. From the time Hilary was a baby, her mom told her about God and his love. But Hilary didn't just hear words about love. Hilary had some hard times as a child; her parents divorced, and the family had struggles to deal with. Yet her mother and stepfather mirrored the love of God to their daughter. In most cases when Hilary messed up, they showed her grace and mercy. When she needed correction, they gave it, but tempered discipline with love. They protected her from harm as best as they could and endeavored to provide what she needed.

> As a father has compassion on his children, so the LORD has compassion on those who fear him.
>
> —PSALM 103:13

When she was four years old, Hilary chose to let God into her heart. And over the next few years, she learned more about God's love through Sunday school classes, children's church, and her mother and stepfather. While she first saw God in the protection, care, and provision of her parents, at some point in her early teen years, she began to experience his love for herself in real-life experiences.

One of these encounters with God happened when she was thirteen, on a two-week mission trip to Ecuador. She had thought God wanted her to go, but the closer it got to her departure date, the more afraid she was. She knew she'd miss her parents terribly; the other team members were older, and she didn't even know them.

As she packed her suitcase, she asked God to be with her because she was scared. Flying out a day early because a huge blizzard was coming in, Hilary only grew more anxious about being out of the country without her parents. But in the midst of her fears, God spoke to her heart, telling her that if she trusted him, he'd be more than faithful.

From the day the team arrived in Riobamba, Ecuador, until the day they left, God kept his promise. Hilary was so busy, there was no time to feel homesick. Mornings were spent building the third floor of a Bible college, and each afternoon she joined the team at an orphanage, telling children about Jesus through songs and skits. Each day God answered specific prayers. It seemed almost as if he was walking with her through the village, showing her that he was her provider, knitting her heart with the other team members, protecting her and keeping her safe while away from her family.

When she felt weak, she was able to lean on God's strength. She felt his hand holding hers and experienced his presence with her. The days flew by, and when it was time to leave, Hilary had been having such a great time, she wasn't ready to go home! She'd tasted what it was like to be used by God to show his love to children who really needed him. Six years later, she can still remember the looks on the faces of the children at the orphanage—at first, always sad and hopeless. But each day, as the team came and loved these children, God used the team's smiles and hugs, broken Spanish, and songs and skits to show the love of the Lord to those who were fatherless.

> Fathers, do not exasperate your children; instead, bring them up in the training and instruction of the Lord.
>
> —EPHESIANS 6:4

Although the family provides the ideal place for a child to grow, flourish in his faith, and develop a sense of how much God loves them, sometimes we (or our child's other parent) mess up. At times we fail to show God's love. Or our child may be hurt or disappointed by life experiences. There's grace for that. As Dr. Ross Campbell says, "We can thank God that his grace is not confined to the good behavior of parents, or many of us would be forever lost."[8]

Helping Your Child Make the Connection

Because we live in a broken world, sometimes we (or someone else) will fail our children. How can we help them deal with the bad as well as the good that comes their way? One way to help your child flow easily into God's love is to connect God to everyday happenings. Saying things like, "I smile when I think of you. Did you know that God smiles when he thinks of you?" or "See how Daddy listened to you? That's how God listens to you, only he doesn't ever sleep, so you can talk to him anytime night or day."

When you blow it, when you've lost your temper, or when your child has received a heart wound,[9] admit your wrong or how you've hurt him and ask your child for forgiveness. Although first apologies may be hard (they're especially hard on our pride), it's worth it to keep short accounts with our children. "As layers of numbness, scarring, or forgetfulness are peeled away, the oil of forgiveness will start to flow, and your hearts will open more and more to each other," says Bruce Wilkinson.[10]

> See what love the Father has given us, that we should be called children of God.
>
> —1 JOHN 3:1 rsv

Even if something disappointing happens, you can point your child to God. "I know this was your weekend to be at your dad's and he promised to pick you up for the zoo but has let you down again. I know you must feel sad, and I'm so sorry you didn't get to go. But God doesn't make promises he doesn't keep. Daddy or I may fail you, but God doesn't. He says here that 'I will never, *never* fail you nor forsake you'" (Heb. 13:5 LB).

If there's been a hurtful incident and a significant person hasn't been loving, acknowledge what's going on, that it hurts, that it is unfair, and by all means, listen to your child's heart. But also point out that that is *not* how God loves her; his love is an unfailing, perfect, eternal love. "The LORD's unfailing love surrounds the man who trusts in him," says David in Psalm 32:10. It may not take the hurt away instantly, but you'll be pointing your child in the right direction—to the Lover of her soul.

At Your Wit's End

Sometimes you may be at your wit's end because you don't have anything left to give. You know your child needs love, and you want to be a good parent, but you're in a bad place—because you're emotionally drained, because your child's behavior is driving you crazy, or maybe just because you're an imperfect human being and you *feel* very unloving.

June was a frustrated mom dealing with a demanding three-year-old whom she didn't even like anymore, much less love. Every day was exhausting. June's daytimer was filled with pediatrician appointments, and her files were full of the test results from trying to find out exactly what was wrong with her son Jamie. He was so demanding, she couldn't leave him with a babysitter. He woke early and tore through the house exploring, taking things apart, or building until well after midnight. ADHD, food allergies, environmental allergies, language deficits—the doctors' list went on and on. Jamie was only three, but his mom felt she'd aged ten years. Frustrated, angry, and depressed, she would whisper faint prayers of desperation, "Help, God; please do something. Make this end."

One day June stood in the kitchen, cleaning in a dazed manner. She'd gone through so much emotionally, she was numb. Then an interesting thought came into her mind. *Start a game. Whenever you feel prompted, call to Jamie and ask, "Guess what?"* June felt compelled to try it, so she yelled up the stairs to her preschooler, "Jamie, guess what?" She had no thought for how she would answer. But when Jamie poked his head around the corner and asked, "What?" the words rolled out of her mouth, "I love you!"

First he looked puzzled, but then he smiled and returned to playing. This game went on for over a week until Jamie answered, "I know what—you love me."

"Yes, but that's not it this time. There's more."

Bounding down the stairs, Jamie asked, "What?"

"Jesus loves you!"

The new game continued for a week until Jamie answered, "I know, you love me and Jesus loves me." As his mom's love and Jesus' love began to soak in, Jamie's behavior began to slowly improve. He was still a challenging child and had difficulties as he began school, but something in his mom's heart, his heart, and God's heart had connected.

> But Jesus said, "Let the little children come to Me, and do not forbid them; for of such is the kingdom of heaven."
>
> —MATTHEW 19:14 nkjv

Today Jamie is a senior in high school. He plays the guitar on the church worship team, has won honors in chess, sports, and science, and has had two consulting jobs with universities (turns out he was gifted in math and science). Jamie knows Jesus loves him, so much so that he asked him to be his Lord and Savior and prays for all his friends. All because God loved his mom so much that he gave her an opportunity to release his love to a little boy he had entrusted to her care. June was looking for an end as a parent, but through his love, God gave her a new beginning.

Every once in a while June still hears those words in her heart, "Guess what?"

And she knows too—God loves her.

Revealing God's Love

God is more than happy to reveal his love to children, and everyday life situations offer opportunities for that to happen. Since Ellen's children are adopted, she reads Scripture verses to them that describe God's hand in their past, present, and future. She teaches them that although she adores them, she can't compare her affection with God's love for them as their *true* father and mother.

When talking about that love, she compares the intangible to the tangible in a fun way: "I love you more than all the bird songs, cricket choruses, and lullabies that have ever been sung." The children turn it into a game, telling Mom they love her more than all the sneezes.

Then Ellen responds, "I love you more than all the water in the ocean, especially if I could turn it into pink lemonade. But God loves you even more! All of my love is only a spark compared to the fireworks of his love for you!"

Mom will be there for them as much and as long as she can, but someday she'll die, she explains. But God will never die, abandon them, or forsake them. Ellen's children are experiencing God's love and protection by the gifts he has already given them—a home, Christian parents, freedom to worship, friends, a beautiful back yard, and nearby parks to play in. But as their mom points them to God, they are also learning to enjoy and love the Giver, not just his gifts.

Opening your own heart to God's love, helping your kids connect God's love to their experiences, and loving your children are all ways to open their hearts to God's unfailing love. I also believe that praying for your children is an essential part of this process. Asking God to reveal his love to them in a way they can understand, praying for the opening of "the eyes of [their] understanding" (NKJV) as Paul described in Ephesians 1:18, and praying for their relationship with the Lord all through their growing-up years is important. If they begin to question God's love as they make the transition from your faith to their own faith in the adolescent years, don't panic— *pray!* Praying for our kids is the greatest influence we can have in their lives. In fact, the prayers of one faithful, persevering mom or dad can change a life, a family, even a nation. Of all the wonderful things we can do for our children, praying for them is at the top of the list of what will have the greatest impact.

> Whenever I am afraid, I will trust in You. In God (I will praise His word), In God I have put my trust; I will not fear.
>
> —PSALM 56:3–4 nkjv

Making the Most of the Loving God Window

As you do some of these activities, which help to open the Loving God Window for your children, remember—we can teach, train, disciple, scold, correct, encourage, but we can't change their hearts. Through prayer, God's Spirit can!

How Are You and God Doing?
(All ages)

"If you're not feeling close to God, guess who moved?" said a sign I once read on a church marquee. Finding out where your kids are with God and how they feel about their relationship with him is a key to helping them connect with God and experience his love. A great way to do that is through art. Get out some white paper and ask your children, "How are you and God doing? How's your relationship?" Encourage them to draw a picture that represents that relationship or to draw a picture of God. Give enough time for drawing, then have each child explain his picture. Next, pray for each other based on what you learned from the drawing. If one of your kids feels close to God and has experienced his love, thank God for that. If another feels distant or is struggling to understand God's love for him, ask how you can pray.

Memorize a Poem about God's Love
(All ages)

This poem would be best for older children; choose a shorter one for young children.

Out in the Fields
with God

by Elizabeth B. Browning

The little cares that fretted me,
I lost them yesterday
Among the fields, above the sea,
Among the winds at play;
Among the lowing of herds,
The rustling of the trees,
Among the singing of the birds,
The humming of the bees.
The foolish fears of what might happen,
I cast them all away
Among the clover-scented grass,
Among the new-mown hay,

Among the rustling of the corn,
Where drowsy poppies nod,
Where ill thoughts die and good are born—
Out in the fields with God.

In the Dark
(Ages 3 and up)

Turn off the lights. Can you see your hand? Your feet? Are they still there? God promises, "I am with you always" (Matt. 28:20 LB). That means that even when it's dark and *you* can't even see yourself, you can be sure that God will keep his promise and be right there with you. Then light several candles. As the light flickers and glows, lighting up the darkness, explain how God is our light—that Jesus is the Light of the World (John 8:12), that his Word lights our path and gives us direction (Ps. 119:105), that there is no place we can go that God's light and glorious presence cannot penetrate (Ps. 139:11–12).

Capitalize on Questions
(Ages 2 and up)

By the time kids can talk well, they begin to ask countless questions like "Who made the moon?" When you answer, "God did," they ask, "Where is God? Who made God?" They are searching to make sense of the world. Use these questions as opportunities to talk about how pets, trees, people, colors, good-tasting food, wonderful smells, clouds and rain, and things all around us are expressions of God's love for us. The Wonder Window chapter has lots of ideas for helping your child's connection with God to grow through simple encounters in nature.

Journal Jots

For Your Child to Write About

• Write what you think about God being with you wherever you go. Was there a time when you were scared? Why? Did you remember God was with you? If you did, did you talk to him? Write what you said.

• What things make you sad? Write them down. Remember that God knows of every time you have cried. He cares for you (1 Peter 5:7).

To Know Him Is to Love Him
(Ages 8 and up)

Remember the old song from the 1960s, "To know, know, know him is to love, love, love him"? That's the way it is with God. To know him is to begin to love him. Take a name of God, such as "God Sees Me," and share with your child the story from the Bible. When

Heart to Heart

Think It Over and Share with Your Child

• Approaching God as a loving Father is easier if you've had a good earthly father. But if your dad missed the mark of God's intention (and to some extent every earthly dad has), seeing God as a loving Father might be more difficult. If you or your children have experienced the absence of a good, loving dad, spend time with the Scriptures (Luke 15:11–32 and John 15:9–12 are good places to start) and talk as a family about the qualities of a good father and how God exhibits those qualities. Then pray that each of you can know and feel his love and affection. If necessary, ask God to help you talk with and/or forgive your earthly father.

• Do you remember a "dark" time in your childhood? Explain to your kids how you felt. If you were a Christian, what did you tell God? How did God bring you comfort? (If you were not yet a Christian, explain how you coped. Remember that it's okay to talk of the security you missed because you didn't know God.)

• Just as Jesus encouraged the little children to come to him, never be too busy to listen to your child's questions or comments. To kids, love is spelled T-I-M-E. Sometimes a child only wants to make a one-sentence comment, but it means the world for kids to be listened to and to have time with you.

Hagar wandered in the desert, an angel sent by God appeared to her. She was promised that God would take care of her and her child. In response, Hagar said to God, "You are [*El Roi*]." *El Roi* means "God who sees me." He sees us when we are sad, when we are lonely, when we are afraid. Kay Arthur whimsically tells Hagar's story in her book *To Know His Name*.[11] (You can check this book out from your local library.) Or read it from the Bible (Gen. 16:7–13). Here's a hands-on project that helps a child understand God as the One Who Sees.

• Draw an eye in the middle of the page. Write under it, El Roi: the God Who Sees. Have your child cut out pictures of people in various settings: in the car, in the kitchen cooking, at the movies. Help paste these pictures around the eye of El Roi. Talk about how God promises never to leave those who trust him (see Psalm 34).

He Is My All
(Ages 6 and up)

Read other names that describe who God is. Do you see how he fills every desire and need we have?

Bookworm

Resources for Children

Davis, Holly. *My Birthday, Jesus' Birthday*. Grand Rapids: Zondervan, 2000. For ages 3–8.

Draper, Dar. *What Is Love?* Sisters, Ore.: Loyal, 2000. For all ages.

God Loves Me Baby Bible Board Book, God Loves Me Bible. Grand Rapids: Zondervan, 1999. For ages 0–3.

Haidle, Helen. *What Did Jesus Promise?* Grand Rapids: Zondervan, 1999. For ages 3–8.

Jacobson, Matt and Lisa. *How Did God Make Me?* Grand Rapids: Zondervan, 1996. For ages 0–9.

Lucado, Max. *Because I Love You*. Wheaton: Crossway, 1999. For all ages.

_____. *You Are Special*. Wheaton: Crossway, 1999. For all ages.

Osborne, Rick, and K. Christie Bowler. *I Want to Know about God: Who God Is, What He Does, and Why He Cares about Me*. Grand Rapids: Zondervan, 1998. For ages 8–12.

Thomas, Mack. *God's Best Promises for Kids*. Colorado Springs: Waterbrook, 1999. For ages 7–12.

- *El Olam:* "God the Everlasting One" or "God of Eternity" (Gen. 21:33)
- *Jehovah-jireh:* "The Lord Will Provide" (Gen. 22:14)
- *Jehovah-rapha:* "The Lord Who Heals" (Ex. 15:22–26)
- *Jehovah-shalom:* "The God of Peace" (Judg. 6:22–24)

(You can find these names of God in Kay Arthur's book *Lord, I Want to Know You.* See Bookbag: Resources for Parents.)

Symbols for Jesus' Name
(Ages 8 and up)

Symbols are forms of communication that have been used for centuries; for instance, early Christians used the symbol of the fish to show they were Christians. Look up the Scripture references in the verses above for some of the names of God. Then create symbols to represent his names.

You Are Safe
(All ages)

The Bible says that the name of God is a strong tower. There is safety and rest in him. Write different names of God on wooden blocks. Construct a tower by gluing the blocks together (it should be big enough in diameter for some Lego-Land or other "people" to go in). Talk about what makes you frightened. Then ask your child what makes him scared. Memorize this comforting verse together: "The name of the LORD is a strong tower; the righteous run to it and are safe" (Prov. 18:10). Take a minute to ask God to remind your child of this verse when fear comes.

Footprints
(Ages 4 and up)

- Read the familiar poem "Footprints." Then pour plaster of paris into a heavy cardboard plate and have your child make a footprint. (Read directions on the bag for proper mixing and setting.)
- List all the familiar places you go: Grandma's house, Dad's business, lake, movie theater, Wal-Mart, mall, grocery store. Title your paper "God Goes with Me."

Even a Sparrow
(All ages)

Jesus says that when a sparrow falls, God knows about it. How much more does he know about what we are experiencing? Go bird-watching. You can get a bird guide from the library. Take along a pad of paper to log your finds; binoculars would be a plus. Learn the birds that are familiar to your region.

Bookbag

Resources for Parents

Arthur, Kay. *Lord, I Want to Know You.* Sisters, Ore.: Multnomah, 1996.

_____. *To Know His Name.* Sisters, Ore.: Multnomah, 1996.

Jesus Is Everything I Need: Challenging Bible Activities on Jesus and All He Is to Us! New York: Warner Brothers, 1998. For ages 8–12.

- Learn to imitate bird-calls
- Keep a record of the various kinds of birds you see in a day
- Study the artwork of John Audubon and read his biography

Throughout your search, remind each other, "You are worth more than many sparrows" (Matt. 10:31).

"Are not two sparrows sold for a penny? Yet not one of them will fall to the ground apart from the will of your Father. And even the very hairs of your head are all numbered. So don't be afraid; you are worth more than many sparrows" (Matt. 10:29–31).

Dry Your Tears
(Ages 6 and up)

"You have collected all my tears and preserved them in your bottle! You have recorded every one in your book" (Ps. 56:8). God wants to comfort us so much that he has even written in a book the times when we were sad and cried. King David remembered this during a troubled time and asked God to save his tears in a bottle. To demonstrate this, get a bottle and have your child decorate it with beads, glitter, or paint. Each time he cries, have him place a drop of water in the bottle. Thank God for his promise to care for you.

Making God's word stick in the heart and mind
of a child is an investment in the future kingdom
of God that will pay hundredfold, maybe
thousandfold in future returns.

—Emmett Cooper, Ph.D., and Steve Wamberg,
Making God's Word Stick

We can trust the Bible to meet children where
they are. We can trust the Bible to point to the God
we know in Jesus the Christ, to make its claims
and announce its promises.

—A. Roger Gobbel and Gertrude G. Gobbel,
The Bible: A Child's Playground

It's important to know that the nurture and admonition
of the Lord is not cramming religion down [a child's]
throat, or a boring daily session of doctrinal instruction.
A child is best trained to love and serve God in an
atmosphere of loving example.
Imagine the impression made on children who
daily hear the Word of God read and explained
by parents who show in voice and attitude that
they believe and respect it.

—Barbara Cook,
How to Raise Good Kids

six

the Bible window

Joy had been reading the book of Mark aloud with her boys over the past four weeks, but now they were ready for the last chapter. In this chapter, Mary Magdalene is weeping at the tomb—hopeless, wondering where her Lord is. Her face is buried in her hands, and through the tears, she sees a pair of feet approach her. "Woman, why are you weeping?" "They've taken him, my Master. Please tell me if you know where he is?" Then a familiar voice says, "Mary." She lifts up her eyes and beholds the face of Jesus.

Joy had read this passage before, but this day as she read it to her sons, the Spirit of God seemed to be sitting with them. She looked up from the pages and met eyes with Isaac, nine; both mother and son had tears. They were filled at that moment with joy and hope; it was a Bible time they won't forget.

Ten-month-old Quinn is too young to talk, so his mom teaches him a Bible verse using hand motions. "Matthew 11:5, the blind receive their sight," she recites with enthusiasm. Quinn's chubby hands cover both his eyes. "And the lame walk." Now each little arm swings in marching motion. Quinn is beginning to hide God's Word in his heart, before he can even say a sentence.

A Parent's Priority

Whether your child is ten months or nine years old, childhood is a prime time to hide God's Word in her heart, help her to know God's love as expressed in the Bible, and help her to understand that the

> From infancy you have known the holy Scriptures, which are able to make you wise for salvation through faith in Christ Jesus. All Scripture is God-breathed and is useful for teaching, rebuking, correcting and training in righteousness, so that the man of God may be thoroughly equipped for every good work.
>
> —2 TIMOTHY 3:15 – 17

Bible is not just a big book without pictures but that it addresses real life. Our kids may learn Bible verses at church, be exposed to God's Word at a Christian school or camp or in Sunday school. But God's instruction to us parents in that familiar Deuteronomy 6 passage is that *we* are to teach God's Word to our children at the breakfast table, as we drive to school, hike in a nature park, and put them to bed at night.

As Dr. Bruce Wilkinson says, "There's no doubt that it is the job of us as parents—not the priests, kings, or prophets—to teach God's truth to our children. Why? Because when our children learn from us, they will more readily move beyond just knowing to obeying."[1]

Exposing your children to Scripture and its validity in everyday living is a vital part of nurturing their walk with God. That's why in this chapter you'll discover ways to bring the wonders of God's Word to life for your growing children so you can help them develop a living faith in a loving God.

Love Letters from God

Reading the Bible is an indispensable aspect of the Christian life. The Bible is God's love letter to his people, young and old. Countless passages describe or demonstrate his love, that love which "was manifested toward us, that God has sent His only begotten Son into the world, that we might live through Him" (1 John 4:9 NKJV).

In addition to telling God's story throughout the ages and proclaiming his unfailing love, the Bible is full of parables to teach children what God and his kingdom are like and hundreds of promises to sustain, comfort, and encourage us. The commands and instructions in God's Word show us how he wants us to live. Besides all that, "the Bible is pure God-given food providing spiritual energy and insight for a lifetime of walking with God."[2]

Second Timothy 3:15–17 says it best, "There's nothing like the written Word of God for showing you the way to salvation through faith in Christ Jesus. Every part of Scripture is God-breathed and useful one way or another—showing us truth, exposing our rebellion, correcting our mistakes, training us to live God's way. Through the Word we are put together and shaped up for the tasks God has for us" (MESSAGE).

Brick by Brick

"Going through a long line of prophets, God has been addressing our ancestors in different ways for centuries. Recently he spoke to us directly through his Son. By his Son, God created the world in the beginning, and it will all belong to the Son at the end. This Son perfectly mirrors God, and is stamped with God's nature. He holds everything together by what he says—powerful words!" says Hebrews 1:1–3 (MESSAGE).

God's powerful words are a prime way for your child to discover and know him, but it doesn't happen all at once. It happens little by little, brick by brick, and precept upon precept, from the time you do high-chair devotions with your toddler to when you tell Bible stories to your first grader, and later as you engage in a discussion with your teen about a difficult passage of Scripture.

But while every part of the Bible is useful and vital to spiritual growth and development, we don't expose young children to the whole thing at once. We need to thoughtfully consider which parts of the Bible to introduce to children at which stages. Just as in the natural world, we give milk to infants and meat to those old enough to chew and digest it. Where do we start?

> Your word is a lamp to my feet and a light for my path.
>
> —PSALM 119:105

For preschool and elementary children, Bible stories are an important way of discovering truth—especially stories that they can relate to, such as stories of baby Jesus and his growing years, Jesus inviting the children to his side to bless them, or Jesus feeding the multitudes with the few fish and loaves of bread a little boy offered. The story of the Good Shepherd holds special interest for kids; they are drawn to the kindness and love of the Shepherd for his sheep, and the parable helps them understand God's love and care for them. The stories of Zacchaeus, the Good Samaritan, David and Goliath, and young Samuel are also engaging for children.

Through Bible stories, children learn that God does powerful things, that he created the world, that he keeps his promises and never fails those who trust and obey him, and a host of other principles for living the Christian life. Even very young children can relate to and treasure the Bible.

> How can a young person live a clean life? By carefully reading the map of your Word.
>
> —PSALM 119:9 message

From the time Tyler was a baby, his mom and dad began reading him stories from his toddler Bible. Filled with big, bright pictures and few words, the toddler Bible is designed to hold the interest of God's littlest people. Now at the age of four, Tyler likes to read out of his two "Big-Boy Bibles" (as he calls them). He carries them to church and enjoys "reading" out of them even if they are upside down. What's amazing is that this preschooler is learning, little by little, the Bible stories and even where some of the books of the Bible are—Genesis and 1 Kings are somewhere near the front.

One night when Tyler was in bed, his parents heard him talking. They listened near his door and peeked in. His little legs were dangling off the side of the bed as he was reading from his Bible. "The kings went up the mountain to get a pail of water," he read. Then he moved on to the story of David and the Giant. He was remembering the story and adding colorful details like how big Goliath's sword was and how mean he was. As his mom stood there, she thought how it must please God to have one of his little children learning more about him, and she felt the importance of continuing to read the Bible to Tyler and encouraging him to "read" it for himself.

Teaching by Example

Nothing demonstrates the importance and value of God's Word to a child quite like the actions of a parent who treasures, reads, and delights in the Bible. When a child sees his dad or mom reading and studying the Bible, he learns to value God's Word. When parents practice biblical principles as a way of life and their actions demonstrate a love for God and his ways, kids see a life worth imitating. As they hear Mom or Dad talk about how the Bible applies to a real-life experience, they are powerfully impacted. Your example is your most powerful tool for influencing your child in any area, whether it's wearing your seatbelt in the car or reading your Bible!

That's because young children are always watching parents and imitating their actions. One day Shenae walked into the den to witness a memorable sight. Tyler had crawled into his daddy's lap to join him in his morning devotions. Together they were saying their prayers. Keith read the Scriptures from his Bible. Tyler, likewise, turned the pages in his Bible until he had found the morning verse, and "read" aloud to his daddy.

> I have hidden your word in my heart that I might not sin against you.
>
> —PSALM 119:11

Even though Keith was in a hurry to get to the office that day, he allowed his son to share in his quiet time with God. He shared a little of what God was doing in his life and what he was thankful for—starting with his son. Tyler felt proud his dad had included him, and Keith was teaching by example the importance of spending time with God. The next morning when Tyler woke up, he came scurrying out of his room with his Bible, ready for devotions. "Where's Daddy?" he asked and ran to find him. He couldn't wait to say hello to God.

Bible Storybooks or Full-Text Bible?

When children are very young, they will enjoy a simple Bible storybook with pictures. Although it is great for children to use Bible storybooks, they should also have direct access to full-text Bibles and hear God's Word being read directly from a parent's Bible. Often adults feel children can't understand the Bible, so they give them only Bible storybooks or little pieces of God's Word in single verses instead of whole passages. However, "it's important to remember that you can experience reality without fully understanding it. That includes the reality of God's Word," says Emmett Cooper. "Children may grasp only a part of its richness and depth—*just as we adults do.* On the other hand, children may show us a new richness and depth because of the way they approach the subject matter."[3]

> Turn my eyes away from worthless things; preserve my life according to your word.
>
> —PSALM 119:37

Here's how one family I know makes the transition from Bible storybook to full-text Bible: from infancy to age four, each child has a beginners Bible or a baby Bible book. The Bible storybooks that take them from Creation to Jesus' resurrection and his return are especially helpful for two- to four-year-olds because they begin to see the bigger picture and how the Bible is a collection of events that relate to each other.

When it's time for family devotions, the child sees the "grown-up" Bible that belongs to Mom and Dad. She and her siblings look in their age-appropriate Bibles (such as the *Kid-Reader Bible* or the *Read to Me Bible,* a full-text Bible with topics of discussion and pictures) and select a story based on the pictures they see. Then Mom and Dad read the story the kids selected, out of the New Living Translation (which they've found is simple enough for even their three-year-old to understand somewhat) or another translation. They might read only for three to five minutes, explain what the passage is saying, and then ask the questions that are in the kids' age-appropriate Bibles for further discussion. By first grade or when children have learned to read, most children will need a full-text Bible for Sunday school. They may still enjoy a Bible storybook to encourage their own reading, but it's time to graduate to a little more grown-up Bible.

By the age of twelve or thirteen, some kids can understand and benefit from nonnarrative portions of the Bible such as Ephesians, Hebrews, or Timothy. Others will catch those books later, maybe in late high school or college. And for all ages, the Proverbs and Psalms are both a blessing and full of instruction and hope.

What about the "hard stuff" in the Bible, when God wipes out his enemies or empowers the Israelites to destroy everyone in the whole city of Jericho—not just wound or injure but kill? How can you handle it when your child asks, "Why did God let all those people die who weren't in the ark with Noah?" This is hard stuff, God's vengeance.

Every child is different, and it takes a parent's sensitivity to her child's heart to know when she is truly ready to learn about the justice and wrath of God. It will challenge your own faith to deal with the hard stuff, especially when you try to help your child understand! It will take prayer and wisdom and perhaps even studying a Bible commentary. You may explain that God didn't create the people of Jericho as enemies. They became enemies of God by the choices they made. God created everyone to have a loving relationship with him, but some people refused his love over and over again. They turned to other gods. He created them and loved them; but they turned their backs on the very God who created them and said, "No, I will not love you." They said this by the way they refused him. Scripture says, "For the wages of sin is death, but the gift of God is eternal life in Christ Jesus our Lord" (Rom. 6:23). That's why God sent his only son, Jesus, to redeem and save people of every tribe and nation, every color and age and race! But there's no easy answer, and there's no magic age when you should introduce these issues. Let the Holy Spirit guide you; ask for wisdom and be assured he will be your teacher as you teach your child.

> I remember your
> ancient laws,
> O LORD, and I find
> comfort in them.
>
> —PSALM 119:52

Creativity Counts

You don't have to be a creative genius to make the Bible come alive for your children. There are numerous ways to build interest in God's Word. Setting familiar Bible stories to music, (like the one below) is a great place to start, even in the car while you're doing errands or on the way to school:

"Noah went and built an ark, God the Father told him so. Animals came two by two, So they would not get all wet. Yes, came the elephant; yes, came the zebras; yes, came the tigers; the Bible tells me so!" to the tune of "Jesus Loves Me" helps kids remember and enjoy the story.

You can also record your child's favorite Bible story on tape (or have Dad or Grandma read it on tape) for those times when you need to concentrate on the traffic. At home, choose a biblical scene like the story of Noah, the Good Samaritan, Jesus calming the wind and the waves, or the Last Supper and have your kids act it out. Describe the setting. Who were the key players? Sketch the story. Let each person take on a speaking role and create dialogue.

Put on an impromptu biblical puppet show by scrunching down behind the couch and let Skip the Dog (or whomever the character is) tell the story of Moses and the Red Sea.

Then after you've presented the story, talk about the "wow!" that comes from realizing truths such as:

- Jesus was so powerful and responded differently to the storm than the disciples because he made everything and was in control of the weather
- God meant it when he said something was going to happen (the flood); the rainbow and his promises are evidence of his faithfulness
- What happened at Jesus' last meal with his disciples
- What the Israelites must have been thinking when the huge waters rolled up and they crossed on dry ground, escaping from the Egyptians

Stand Firm!

Another way to hide God's Word in your child's heart and help bring understanding and application of its truths is to use movement and everyday objects. Lisa, a Mississippi mom, had been fascinated with her personal study of passages in the Bible that talked about trees. She decided to take one of those verses, 1 Corinthians 15:58, which reads, "Therefore, my dear brothers, stand firm. Let nothing move you," and teach her son Trace the meaning of that verse.

As they walked on a golf course one Sunday afternoon, she asked Trace to go over to a particular tree and push it, to try as hard as he could to move it. She convinced him that as big and strong as he was, he should at least try. Trace gave it all he had and then said, "Mom, I can't move this tree. I tried as hard as I could and it is *not* going to move."

Lisa knelt down and said, "Trace, Jesus told us to be just like that tree. He told us to stand firm and not move from what we know is right. Would you stand like a tree, with your arms down beside you and your feet firmly planted on the ground?" Trace responded by being the firmest planted tree he could be.

"Okay, if someone walks up to you and says, 'Come on, Trace, let's go push the girls down on the playground' what are you going to do?" While she said this to him, she acted as if she was trying to push him as he had tried to push the tree.

Trace didn't move and said, "No, I don't want to."

"Trace, let's act silly during music class instead of singing like the teacher said. If we get caught, they'll only put us in time-out again," Lisa said. Again, she tried to push him as she was talking, and again, he didn't move. "No, the teacher told us not to!" Trace responded.

> The unfolding of your words gives light; it gives understanding to the simple.
>
> —PSALM 119:130

His mom was thrilled. She could tell he understood exactly what it meant to stand like a tree—to stand firm. Now when he gets out of the car at school, all she has to say is, "Trace, be a tree today!"

Games are another way Lisa has found to teach spiritual truths. Twister is one of their favorites. They get all twisted up, with right foot on blue, left hand on yellow, left foot on green. As the game moves on, the players get all tangled up in knots and end up falling down because they can't support themselves any longer. Then Lisa shares how the Lord can keep us from falling if we build our lives on him (see Ps. 46:5 and Matt. 7:24–25) and how he strengthens us when we are tangled up in the stresses and strains of life. And when we do fall, he is there to catch us (see Ps. 37:23–24).

Each of these are simple, inexpensive, but dynamic methods to help the Bible come alive for children that will bear fruit as God's Word is hidden in their hearts. Having a Bible time each day with your children will do more than you would imagine to help them develop the habit of reading what God's Book has to say. If it's important for *you* to hear from God's Word daily, how much more important is it for your children whose hearts need to be protected and turned toward the Lord?

You may not see the fruit of your efforts until somewhere down the road, but it's worth the investment. Paula and Larry Dinkins, missionaries in Thailand, shared with me how setting aside time for God's Word made a difference in their family. They started when their oldest child, Andy, was almost four. Sitting on their teakwood sofa, Larry holding Andy, and Paula holding their two-year-old, they read one verse a day from a devotional booklet for kids aged three to six. After their next two children came along, they would put the breakfast dishes aside after cereal was eaten and juice consumed (or spilled) and read a Bible verse and a page from a devotion. Then each of the six family members prayed a short prayer of thanksgiving or intercession for each other and the concerns of the day. Little did they know how this would influence their children's lives. Now in college, their two oldest begin their days with God and his Word even though they are thousands of miles away from the family.

The Big Key

When you read the Bible to your child, don't forget to help her see how the Scriptures apply to real life today. That way she sees that it's not just for people back in biblical times but is relevant for her life. As Søren Kierkegaard said, "When you read God's Word, you must constantly be saying to yourself, 'It is talking to me, and about me.'"

One dad I know does that by telling his children Bible stories when he's taking them to school or sports. If one of them is struggling with a problem or worry, he'll pick out a person from the Bible who had the same struggle and tell him that story, pointing out how God helped in a mighty way. The kids not only remember these stories but also have grown into a greater appreciation of God's Word and how it applies to their lives.

When you read the Bible with your kids, look for Scriptures that address problems or issues they are facing. Ask questions like, "So what does this verse mean?" and "How does it apply to you in your life, school, or sports?" Help your kids realize that as we grow, we can get something new from the same passage we've read dozens of times, because we're at a different place. The Bible is *that* good! (And if you can give them an example of a verse that hit you differently when you were married than when you were in high school or college, this will really hit home.)

The little-by-little approach works well for helping children memorize Bible verses. Try taking a verse a week to put in their memory banks, and in a year, they will know fifty-two golden nuggets of truth. Verses they learn in childhood are treasures that will yield benefits both now and later. Use different approaches for memorizing Scripture. One of your children may memorize Bible verses best by repeating them aloud. Some memorize better by setting the verse to music. Using

> Your word, O LORD, is eternal; it stands firm in the heavens.
>
> —PSALM 119:89

songs and music is a powerful memorization tool—whether setting a verse to a familiar tune or listening to a CD of psalms or Scripture choruses—because music is processed on the right side of the brain and language is processed on the left side of the brain. If you put the two together—words and music—you have a stronger imprint on the memory and better recall later.

You can also help your child recognize spiritual principles operating in your day-to-day lives. If your flowers wilt because of the heat and then perk up and return to a vibrant state after you water them, share with your child that there's always hope with God and things can be restored if we trust in him. Or discuss how God's Word waters our hearts and helps us stay spiritually alive. Then share a verse like Psalm 42:5, "Fix my eyes on God—soon I'll be praising again" (MESSAGE).

A candle holds a world of possibilities for spiritual understanding. When you light a candle, share with your child that this is how God wants our lives to be—a lighthouse to those around us who may be in darkness. Verses such as "Let your light so shine before men" (Matt. 5:16 NKJV) and "You are the light of the world" (Matt. 5:14), suddenly have more meaning.

In the early years, and throughout childhood, you can fill your children's minds with God's stories, instructions, and wisdom. Along the way, they will discover how much God loves them. It's not difficult if you do it little by little and follow Deuteronomy's advice to teach your kids when you sit at home and when you walk along the road, when you lie down and when you get up.

Making the Most of the Bible Window

Motion Memory
(Ages 3 and up)

Take a Bible verse and make up hand motions to it with your kids (or use sign language if you know it). Children seem to respond deeply to signing, and the signs can help them worship God with their whole being. Here are a couple of examples:

Matthew 11:5	
The blind receive sight,	Cover eyes with both hands.
the lame walk,	Now swing arms in marching motion.
those who have leprosy are cured,	Place both arms across chest and then
the deaf hear,	place hands over ears; release.
the dead are raised,	Hide head in lap; pop up.

and the good news is preached to the poor.	Form a Bible with both hands and move it.

Psalm 34:1–3	
I will [bless] the LORD at all times;	Point to wrist where your watch would be.
his praise	Clap your hands.
will always be on my lips.	Point to mouth.
My soul will boast in the LORD;	Stick thumbs to chest.
let the afflicted hear	Cup hand by ear.
and rejoice.	Wide grin; extend hands under chin to represent a glow.
Glorify the LORD with me	Raise hands to sky.
let us exalt his name together.	Clap hands.

Telling the Stories with Bible Figures
(Ages 2–8)

Just as you use Nativity characters to tell the Christmas story, utilize whatever Bible-time characters or felt-board characters you can gather. You can tell the Bible stories with them, and then your children can touch and move the figures while telling and retelling the stories in their own words and way. Noah and the ark and animals to tell the story of the flood and a shepherd and sheep for telling the Good Shepherd parable are two examples.[4]

Enhancing Wonder in God's Word
(Ages 2–7)

"Wondering together produces thinking Christians who can enter into dialogue, share their experience of God, and together discover God's calling for them," write Stewart and Berryman in *Young Children and Worship*.[5] Wonder questions (I wonder what Peter felt like when he walked on the water; I wonder how Noah felt when the rain poured down) are much better for young children than fact or detail questions (How many brothers did Joseph have?). Wonder questions help children ponder and meditate on the meaning of the story and give them a chance to experience God instead of just being told about God. In your personal Bible time, jot in the margin a few wonder questions to ask and talk about with your child.

Pray the Bible
(All ages)

Have your child choose a favorite verse, write it on an index card, then change it into a prayer and pray it back to God. Have your child personalize the verse by putting in his own name and using personal pronouns. Verses from the Psalms (especially short ones) are especially well-suited for children because they are direct, heartfelt, honest requests and praise sentences. For example: "How great is the Lord!" (Ps. 13:5 LB). Or you can talk to God using a Bible verse. "Lord, you said that nothing is impossible with God [see Luke 18:27], but today everything seems impossible. Please help me believe in you and your power!"

Scripture Sketch
(All ages)

Together with your child, illustrate Matthew 11:5. Imagining and drawing pictures make a big impression and help the verses go into long-term memory. Here is an example:

The blind receive sight,	a sad face with lines (or blinders) for eyes; a smiley face
the lame walk,	man sitting down; man jumping in the air
those who have leprosy are cured,	man with spots; a man without
the deaf hear	man yelling into another's ear, a question mark above him; both men talking to each other

the dead are raised,	man on cot, people around are crying; man sits up
and the good news is preached to the poor.	man teaching from Bible to a crowd

Ask Curious Bible Questions
(Ages 4 and up)

A great way to discover what's in your child's heart and to share your thoughts without your child feeling like you're lecturing her is to play Curious Bible Questions. Try conversation-starters like:

- If Jesus had come during our lifetime and asked you to be a disciple, would you have dropped everything to follow him or would you have felt that you had to finish your soccer game or homework?
- If you could be any Bible character, who would you be and why?
- Do you believe in miracles? Have you ever experienced a miracle?
- Have you ever seen an angel?
- God made the whole world. If you could visit anywhere in the world, where would you go?

Devotions with Little Ones
(Ages 1–5)

Keep devotions with toddlers and preschoolers short and simple. Have a worship or quiet-time box. For kids under two years old, the box can

Heart to **H**eart

Think It Over and Share with Your Child

- Share with your child a favorite Bible verse or one that has special meaning for you. Tell him what you experienced that made that passage special.
- Tell your child of an incident that made you relate better to a Bible character. What was the situation? Did you respond the same way that he or she did in Scripture? How did God help you through that time?

contain toys and Bible figures especially reserved for daily devotional times. Add crayons and paper for two- and three-year-olds, and a few

Bookworm

Resources for Children

Beers, V. Gilbert. *Step by Step Bible*. Colorado Springs: Chariot Victor, 1999. For ages 8 and up.

Josh and the Big Wall—Playset, VeggieTales. A great way for your 4- to 7-year-olds to reenact the Joshua story, VeggieTales style.

New Explorer's Study Bible for Kids. Nashville: Nelson, 1999. For ages 8–12.

NirV Read to Me Bible for Kids. Broadman and Holman. Tailored to preschoolers. Includes "Spiritual Truths for Children," which shows you when kids are most capable of learning specific principles.

Peek-a-Bible interactive storybooks. Grand Rapids: Zondervan. For ages 6 and under. Includes *The Big Boat Ride*, *Jonah Goes Overboard*, *The Lost and Found Lamb*.

Bruno, Bonnie and Carol Reinsma. *The Young Reader's Bible*. Cincinnati: Standard, 1998. For ages 6–10

Rice, Wayne, and David R. Heerman. *Reality 101: What the Bible Says to Teens about Real-Life Questions*. Wheaton: Tyndale House, 1999. For ages 13 and up.

Rock, Louis. *The Ten Commandments for Children*. Colorado Springs: Cook Communications, 2000. For all ages.

Taylor, Kenneth. *My First Bible*. Wheaton: Tyndale House, 1999. For preschoolers and beginning readers to read to themselves.

Woody, Marilyn J. High Chair Devotions series. Colorado Springs: Chariot/Victor. Includes *God Cares for Me, God Gave Me a Gift, God Is My Friend, God Made My World*. For all ages.

silk flowers and small stuffed dogs and horses for when you sing about God creating gardens and animals. Include music, Bible stories, simple prayers, and many hugs to make early encounters with God memorable and positive.

Sing a Psalm
(Ages 2–11)

Select a Scripture verse and put it to music; the tune could be from a favorite hymn, nursery rhyme, or other song. Teach a song like "This is the day, this is the day, that the Lord has made, I will rejoice, I will rejoice and be glad in it" to memorize Psalm 118:24.

Pocket Prompts
(Ages 2–11)

Have each child write a Bible verse on an index card. They can decorate the cards with stickers, markers, and a drawing that prompts their memory about the meaning of the verse. Have a "Scripture draw" to see how fast they can pull out their card, hand it to you, and quote the verse (or as much of it as they know). Take these Pocket Prompts in the car and have the kids quiz each other, remembering to review previously memorized verses.

Even two- and three-year-olds can learn simple memory verses such as "Be kind one to another" (Eph. 4:32 NKJV), "Love one another" (John

Journal Jots

For Your Child to Write About

• Write down your thoughts on how the Creator of the universe shows his love for you. How does that help you love the kid nobody else likes?

• The Living Bible, the Phillips translation of the New Testament, and the Message are what we call "paraphrase" versions rather than translations of the Bible. The writers were attempting to put the Bible into our modern-day language to make it understandable. Have your child take a verse and make up her own paraphrase by putting it in words her peers would understand.

13:34), and "Children, obey your parents" (Eph. 6:1 LB).

Bookbag

Resources for Parents

Cooper, Emmett, and Steve Wamberg. *Making God's Word Stick.* Nashville: Nelson, 1996.

Jacobson, Matt and Lisa Jacobson. *The Big Ten for Little Saints.* Sisters, Ore.: Loyal, 2000. The timeless truths of God's Ten Commandments applied to kids' real lives.

The Memorizer, Bible Memory Plan (with Unique Memory Books, Incentives and Accountability). Scripture Memory Fellowship. 314-569-0244; memorize@slnet.com or www.scripturememory.com

The Singing Bible. Focus on the Family. Heritage Builders Resources. 1-800-A-FAMILY.

Wise Guy
(Ages 5–11)

Decorate a big chair as a throne. Make a crown out of cardboard, glitter, and markers (you can also make a scepter and signet ring if your kids are feeling creative) and choose a "king." Have the "people of the land" come to ask Bible questions from a Bible trivia game or make up your own questions. If the king can't answer the question, then the first to answer inherits the throne. Talk about the kings of the Bible. Read about the wisdom of Solomon (2 Chron. 9:1–8) and the humility of David while King Saul still ruled (1 Sam. 24).

Mysterious Metaphors
(Ages 8 and up)

Metaphors liken one object to another. The Bible is a gold mine of metaphors!

- Jesus, the Lamb: "In a loud voice they sang: 'Worthy is the Lamb, who was slain, to receive power and wealth and wisdom and strength and honor and glory and praise!'" (Rev. 5:12).

  Ponder why Christ would be called a lamb. (Look in Exodus 12:1–11, 43–51 when the Passover lamb was prepared. Compare offering a lamb for the Passover meal to what Christ did for us on the cross.)

Do you know any songs that speak of Jesus being the Lamb?

• Christ, the rock: "He alone is my rock and my salvation" (Ps. 62:2).

Do you know any songs about Christ being the rock? For instance, "The Wise Man Built His House upon the Rock," "Upon This Rock," and "My Hope Is Built on Nothing Less." Why is Jesus described as a rock?

Accentuate the Positive
(All ages)

For most of the negative things in our lives, we say or think that God's Word has a positive for it. As you're reading the Bible with your child, start a list of these positives and you'll be helping to renew your child's mind in the truth. Try Philippians 4:13 when your child says, "I can't do it" or Luke 18:27 when he says, "It's impossible." Second Timothy 1:7 is a great antidote for fear, 1 Corinthians 1:30 works when he says, "I'm not smart enough," and John 13:34 is good for when he says, "No one loves me."

As a child runs to his father and tells him everything in the days when he is very young and very innocent and very trusting, so we can talk to God.

—William Barclay

Every evening, when my mum has turned out my light, I pray to God, telling him everything (though not in as much details as adults!), asking him to protect people, requesting help or forgiveness. At times like these, I feel especially close to God and feel really as if he's my friend, and I can pour out my troubles and worries.

—Sarah, 10

Though her voice is small and mild, all Heaven stills for the prayers of a child!

—Anonymous

Kids see God "with skin on" when Mom and Dad pray about a financial problem instead of panicking, when they show love to a hurting family with a practical act of kindness, when they forgive a child who just hurt them, when they often stop and give thanks for good things that happen, when they talk more about the blessings than the complaints.

—Ron Hutchcraft,
Five Needs Your Child Must Have Met at Home

seven

the **prayer** window

"Justin, would you pray tonight?" I asked our son when his family was over for dinner. Sitting in her high chair, our granddaughter Caitlin, two, clasped her little hands, bowed her head, and joined us. When the prayer was finished, she said, "Amen!" and, with a big smile, suggested, "Let's pray again!" Caitlin enjoys prayer just as she enjoys eating with the family, reading with us, blowing bubbles, or doing any number of other activities. It's just a part of her life.

Ever since Caitlin could barely talk, every night as she goes to bed and her mommy or daddy say evening prayers with her, she lays her head down and prays for everybody in the family, in her own way—God bless Nandy (that's me), Pa-Pa, June (her great-grandmother), Aunt Ali, Uncle Hans, Chris, Maggie, Mimi, Mother Kitty, Joy, and all the pets in the extended family. Caitlin's prayers are very simple and concise, but the God of the universe is attuned to her little voice.

Like Caitlin, children who are introduced to God early in life, who have praying parents, and who grow up in a home where talking to God is normal, begin to understand that God is someone with whom they can share their thoughts, hurts, and needs. That's because the early years are a time in life when talking to God comes naturally and conversations are unhindered by religious conventions or stilted language. Children can learn to pray before they learn to read, ride a bike, or tie their shoes. They don't have to wait

> Let the little children come to me! Never send them away! For the Kingdom of God belongs to men who have hearts as trusting as these little children's. And anyone who doesn't have their kind of faith will never get within the Kingdom's gates.
>
> —LUKE 18:16–17 lb
> (SEE ALSO MATT. 19:14)

until they start school or grow up. Very young children can be taught to offer simple one- or two-sentence prayers at mealtime and bedtime, to memorize short prayer sentences from the Bible, to turn to God and talk to him throughout their day.

Kids, unlike adults, don't have to be in church or in their quiet-time place at a certain time of day to pray. At school (especially during tests; test times are the one time they'll never be able to outlaw prayer), at play, in bed when the lights are out, all are perfect places and times to talk to God. And children who are encouraged to pray when they're young begin to connect with God in a real way, to know him, not just know about him, as they grow.

"I feel really close to God when I ride my bike. I just spill all my thoughts out. Sometimes I make up songs and sing to him. Or just talk. I think it's the best time of day," says Chelsea, eleven.

Even a bad day can be a vehicle for connecting with God. "I feel God's presence most when I've just had an argument or am feeling down. I tell God how I feel, then think how the other person must feel or might feel. Then I realize what I did wrong and say sorry and ask forgiveness. Usually I feel better and either say I'm sorry or read and say I'm sorry later," explains Fiona, ten.

Prayer: Simply Talking with God

"Prayer is being with God," writes Calvin Miller in his book *Into the Depths of God*.[1] Our kids need to know early in their lives that they can talk to God just like they'd talk to Mommy, Daddy, or a best friend. That he's there and attentive to what they have to say. Instead of putting them on hold or playing a recorded message, God is always willing to listen—whether they're in the car, on the playground, at a friend's house, or in Sunday school. They understand this concept of God's willingness to interact with them through prayer, from parents who lead them not only in mealtime and bed-time prayers but also in spontaneous prayers.

One day Linda was driving with her two children in Chiang Mai, Thailand (where they serve as missionaries), when they saw a motor-scooter wreck—a very common occurrence in Thailand—and an ambulance speeding up to the scene. Linda slowed the car down at the first opportunity, stopped, and said, "Lord, would you take care of those people who got hurt? Would you go ahead of them to the hospital and give the doctors wisdom and comfort the family?" Then she resumed driving.

With that simple prayer, which took only a few moments, Linda demonstrated to her children her belief that God is present with them, that he's listening when they pray, and that he cares about everything in their lives and others' lives too. When Linda's husband is abnormally late getting home from somewhere, when he has an important speaking engagement or meeting, when Linda can't find something she's looking for or needs direction, she prays spontaneously and audibly in the car or at home. And her children are beginning to do the same.

His ears are attentive to their prayer.

—I PETER 3:12

Modeling: The Best Way for Kids to Learn to Pray

Kids learn the importance of prayer by hearing their parents pray and by watching the prayer process. (And they are watching us all the time.)

Ever since Joshua was born, prayers have been a part of his bed-time routine. When he was just an infant, his dad would pray over him each night, asking for God's protection and for God's love to fill his heart. When Josh was eighteen months old, his parents added a short nightly reading from his toddler's Bible to their brief prayer time.

Then at two years of age, Josh joined in by looking around his room and naming everything he could see to thank God for.

"Thank you God for my blankets, puppy, Mommy, Daddy, new shoes, light, eyes, ears, nose, boogers . . ." He thanked God for the most interesting items! But it wasn't only Josh that was growing spiritually during their prayer times. Hearing her son's simple prayers, his mom couldn't remember the last time she had thanked God for her shoes, eyes, ears, nose, and all the other simple blessings in her life. Through her son, she was reminded of all she had to be thankful for.

> The moment you began praying, a command was given. I am here to tell you what it was, for God loves you very much.
>
> —DANIEL 9:23 lb

"The best way for a child to learn to pray is to live with a father and mother who know a life of friendship with God and who truly pray," said eighteenth-century writer Johann Heinrich Pestalozzi. Modeling a lifestyle of prayer for your child will have a powerful, long-lasting impact because kids learn the most from what they see us do in the course of our everyday lives. Children "catch" prayer from parents who talk and listen to God, are enthusiastic about praying with and for others, and share prayer with their kids in both the crises and ordinary times of family life.

Teach a Prayer Model

Have you ever asked a child to pray and he responded, "But I don't have anything to say"? For kids age eight and up, I've found that a prayer model like the Four Steps of Prayer makes talking to God easier. Before age seven or eight, kids' prayers are mainly prayers of thanksgiving and praise, so use caution. If your child is thanking God, don't quickly switch gears and tell him to pray about a problem. Be led by the Spirit and attuned to your child's heart. Listen to his prayers and allow for silence and pauses.

We don't have to be rigid about following a prayer model such as the Four Steps—think guidelines, not formula—but it can give structure and help to focus our thoughts. Here are the four steps:

Praise

"You are the best and full of glory!" Christina, nine, said. "You are the most awesome, wonderful God. I love you!" Morgan, seven, said. In praise, we tell God how much we love him and focus on who he is, not just on what he can do for us. Starting our prayer focused on God instead of our problems helps us gain perspective. The problems don't seem as big; God can handle them and us. This is just as important for kids as for adults, because a child's problems of not having a friend or not understanding his math and failing the test can seem overwhelming at times.

Spending a few minutes praising God by reading aloud verses from Psalms (try Psalms 92; 98; 100; 101; 115; or 114–150) will jumpstart your praise. The Psalms are simple, direct, sincere expressions of praise, so they're perfect for kids. You can take a selection and personalize it: "When I am afraid, I will hide under your wings. You will protect me from anyone who would want to hurt me. You are a mighty God. I want to tell everyone how wonderful you are!" or "I will sing happy songs to you. I will sing and tell everyone how wonderful you are. I see everything you made all around me. You made the trees, flowers, birds, dogs, cats, and people. You are all-powerful. I praise your name!"[2]

> And whoever receives one such child in My name receives Me.
>
> —MATTHEW 18:5 nasb

As you encourage your kids to enter into praise, they'll get a fresh glimpse of who God is, which is one of the biggest blessings of prayer.

Confession

No matter what our age, a key component in prayer is confession. You can explain it this way: God longs to hear from his children, but sometimes the lines of communication get clogged up with unconfessed sin, anger, unforgivingness, wrong actions, or a variety of offenses we commit. Confession reopens the communication lines so we can hear God as we pray and so God can hear us. David said in Psalm 66:18, "If I had cherished [or harbored or held on to] sin

in my heart, the Lord would not have listened." Our kids need to
know that!

"Create in me a clean heart, O God," (Ps. 51:10) can help you
begin. Ask your children, "What are some of the wrong things we do
that grieve God—words or deeds that we might need to tell God
about?" Then encourage them to silently
confess whatever comes to mind. Children
tend to be much more honest and open

**And He took them
up in His arms, laid
His hands on them,
and blessed them.**

—Mark 10:16 nkjv

about their wrongdoings than adults, and
quicker to confess them as well, so they may
end up leading you in this part of the
prayer. (Admitting when we're wrong and
asking for forgiveness is great modeling.)

John, a third-grade student, was kept in
class during recess and required to do a
writing assignment because of his misbehavior. On his paper he wrote, "God, would
you forgive me for my sins, because you are holy, you are awesome,
you will hear my prayer. Please forgive me! I was wrong to push the
kids and be mean on the playground." At a young age, he understood the principle of coming to God to admit our wrongdoings and
experienced the freedom of being forgiven.

Thanksgiving

An essential part of prayer is simply saying, "Thank you, God."
With a little nudging, children enjoy being specific about what
they're grateful for, often going on longer with thanksgiving than we
think we have time for. Ask what blessings God has given them or
the best thing in their day and then have each child share. Besides
verbalizing, writing blessings in a family journal is a terrific way to
record blessings and answers to prayer so that you can remember
the Lord's goodness.

Intercession

Intercession means standing in the gap (or in the need of prayer)
for someone else; it's like bringing your friend by the hand to the

throne of grace for God's help. We can pray for our own needs, our children's needs, and the needs of others. A creative way Debby, a Virginia mom, mobilizes her four kids to pray for others takes only five minutes a day.

After breakfast each morning, the family focuses on one group or one person to pray for during the five-minute intercession time. On Mondays, it's missionaries. (Each child will pick a missionary they want to pray for.) On Tuesday, it's two friends. On Wednesday, it's somebody who's not a Christian or a part of the world that's unreached. Thursday is Thankful Day. They don't ask for anything; they just thank God. Friday is for praying for family—each other or someone in the extended family. In just five minutes a day, the children are learning to care enough about others to bring them to God in prayer and ask him to bless them and help them.

Prayer Connects You, Heart to Heart

One of the wonderful things about sharing prayer times with your children is that it not only connects your child's heart to God, but it will connect you and your child, heart to heart. In our fast-paced lifestyles in which well-meaning families can become fragmented, with parents going in one direction and kids in another, a close connection is desperately needed. Think about someone with whom you've shared and prayed with over time and the intimacy and closeness that develops. That kind of close relationship and sharing is vital for parents and children, and prayer can be a vehicle for it to happen. As you pray together, you'll understand your kids' real concerns, the things that worry them, and what they care most about. They'll feel cared for and loved.

> Don't worry about anything; instead pray about everything; tell God your needs and don't forget to thank him for his answers.
>
> —PHILIPPIANS 4:6 lb

Your children will also see God act and will begin to know his faithfulness in their lives as prayers are answered. Their faith and yours will grow as you see God work.

Ever since Sarah was six years old, she told her parents that she felt a call to be a missionary singer. One evening when she was eight, she called her dad to her bedside.

"What do you want?" he demanded in the frustrated tones of a tired dad.

"Daddy," Sarah pleaded. "How can I be a missionary singer when I grow up if I have no piano to practice on?"

"We don't have money to buy a piano," her dad retorted. "Pray about it, see what God will do, and *get to sleep!*" He didn't feel much like a loving Christian dad at that moment, but he did point his daughter in the right direction. Sarah prayed that evening. The next morning a family from their church called, saying, "God has been dealing with us about helping you to buy a piano so that Sarah can take lessons." Later that day, another family called with the same message. This eight-year-old had prayed with confident, believing faith, and God came through miraculously. That provision of a piano became part of Sarah's history with God. Now Sarah, a recent graduate of Evangel University in Springfield, Missouri, is serving as a music teacher in one of the largest mission fields on planet earth: the public school system. And they still have her baby grand piano in the family room, a reminder of God's faithfulness.

What about When God Says "Wait" or "No"?

As much as we'd like it, our kids' prayers aren't all answered as quickly as Sarah's. Sometimes they pray and pray and nothing happens. Sometimes God closes a door in spite of their earnest prayers or his answer seems to be no. How can we help them deal with unanswered prayers?

Sometimes we think God hasn't answered our prayers unless we receive what we want (when we want it). But God is not a genie, and prayer is not rubbing a magic bottle. God answers all our prayers— sometimes yes, sometimes wait, and sometimes no. When he says no or answers differently than we expect, we may be as frustrated and angry as our child!

Instead of avoiding the subject, together with your child think of people in the Bible to whom God said no, such as Job, Jeremiah,

Jesus, and Paul. What can we learn from their experiences and how they responded to God in the midst of their struggles?

Think of a time when you received a no or a disappointing result from your prayers, only to discover that God knew best and later brought something better or showed his grace through the situation in a way you couldn't have imagined. Share with your children what you learned from that experience. Help them see that while God's ways are not our ways and there is much we won't entirely comprehend until heaven, he does urge us to ask, and whatever the answer, they can always trust his love even when they can't understand why something is happening.

Learning to Listen

Because conversation is always a two-way street—listening as well as talking—a key thing we want our kids to know is how to tune in and listen to God. We can demonstrate the importance of listening in simple ways, even with young children.

"Mommy, how does God speak to us?" five-year-old Grace asked her mom. Carol, her mother, explained that sometimes God speaks to us through his Word, sometimes in prayer, sometimes through other people, and sometimes he may speak directly to us with a thought, and if so, it's important to do what he says.

> The prayer of a person living right with God is something powerful to be reckoned with.
>
> —JAMES 5:16 message

A few days later during a family devotion time, Grace said she wanted to pray for Ning-Ning, their former housekeeper, who was living thousands of miles away. They hadn't talked to Ning-Ning for months, but Grace prayed for her that night. At the next prayer time, she asked to pray for her again. That night the family received an e-mail from a friend telling them that Ning-Ning had been beaten up on the first night that Grace felt impressed to pray for her. It was a precious moment as Grace realized that God had spoken to her, leading her to intercede for Ning-Ning, and she had obeyed him. Prayer became more meaningful as they took time to listen to God.

By modeling prayer, engaging your children in daily prayer times, praying spontaneously, and helping your kids learn to listen to God, your kids will grow more and more to know God, not just know about him from worksheets in Sunday school. They will know that he loves them with an everlasting, unconditional love. They'll know there is a friend who will be with them forever but who is very much present and available at every moment and that he wants to speak to them and guide them throughout their lives on earth. Prayer can become as natural as breathing. Then when you aren't there and they're at high school or college and have a problem, they will know whom to turn to—a loving God who listens, cares, and acts on their behalf.

Making the Most of the Prayer Window

Short and Sweet
(Ages 0–5)

For very young children, short, enjoyable prayer times of five minutes or less are better than extended sessions in prayer. Avoid pushing little ones into prayer times that exceed their attention span. Prayer is a language of the heart and can't be forced or manipulated. The prayers of young children tend to be short, primarily consisting of a few words of thanks or praise: "Thank you, Jesus, for baby brother" or "Thank you for making the world." Aim for short conversational prayers, with a generous dose of warmth, realness, and heart-to-heart spontaneity when you pray with toddlers and preschoolers.

Pray through the Newspaper
(Ages 7 and up)

You can turn the daily newspaper into a prayer journal. Pass out sections to your kids and ask each to come up with one concern from the articles in their section that you could pray about.

Musical Mealtime Prayers
(All ages)

To familiar tunes, like "Where Is Thumpkin," you can thank God for food: "God our Father, God our Father, once again, once again, thank you for our blessings, thank you for our blessings. Amen. Amen."

Pray on the Spot
(All ages)

The next time your child comes to you with a problem or worry, instead of saying, "I'll pray for you," do it right then. Even if it's a short prayer, you'll be sharing the important principle that God wants us to cast the care of all our concerns on him and to pray about everything.

Memorize the Lord's Prayer
(Ages 3–6)

Heart to Heart

Think It Over and Share with Your Child

- Share with your child a time that you prayed and received the answer in a dramatic or surprising way.
- Has God ever spoken to you before? If so, what did he say and how did you respond? Share with your children the ways you've found to hear God.

Although conversational praying is great, for kids who are reluctant to pray aloud, it can help to memorize a prayer. Even three- and four-year-olds can memorize a short prayer like "Now I lay me down to sleep" or "God is great, God is good, and we thank him for this food" as a starter and springboard. One of the best prayers for a child to memorize is the Lord's Prayer in Luke 11:2–4, as it can be a jump-start to meaningful, personal prayer. Within the Lord's Prayer are the elements of praise, thanksgiving, forgiveness, protection, and direction. Go through each part with your child, perhaps having them draw a picture of what the key words mean, and pray the Lord's Prayer in family devotions from time to time.

Pray a Blessing
(All ages)

Praying a prayer of blessing on your child's life each night at bedtime can bring comfort, reassurance, and hope to your child's heart. Before your child leaves for school, a sleepover at a friend's house, camp, or other "firsts," pray a blessing. *Blessing* actually means to invoke God's divine favor on someone. Put your hand on your child's head or shoulder and pray for God's favor, protection, and peace. Or use a Bible blessing such as Psalm 5:12 or Numbers 6:25. When you pray scriptural blessings, you are speaking words that match God's desire for your child's purpose and destiny.

Pondered
(Ages 8 and up)

Study the prayers of great men and women of the centuries (see Bookshelf: Resources for Parents for book suggestions): political figures like George Washington, theologians or ministers like Peter Marshall, scientists like George Washington Carver.

Look at prayers in the Bible. Besides the prayers of Jesus, read David's prayer for blessing in 2 Samuel 7:18–29; Elijah's prayer in 1 Kings 18:36–37; Jehosophat's prayer

---

Bookworm

Resources for Children

Haidle, Helen. *Comfort for a Child's Heart.* Grand Rapids: Zondervan, 1999. For ages 3–8.

Miller, Steve. *A Child's Garden of Prayers.* Eugene, Ore.: Harvest House, 1999. For ages 5–10.

Nappa, Mike. *52 Fun Family Prayers.* Minneapolis: Augsburg, 1996. For all ages.

Patterson, Edwina. *God Has Big Ears.* Plano, Tex.: Heart for the Home, 1999. Daily devotional flip calendar with prayer thoughts for children ages 3–10, all based on Scripture. 1-800-344-8022.

_____. *Praise Praying from the Psalms for Children: With Examples of Prayers for Children and Parents.* Plano, Tex.: Heart for the Home, 1998. 1-800-344-8022. For ages 4–10.

Smith, Debbie and Michael W. Smith. *Where's Whitney?* Grand Rapids: Zondervan, 2000. For ages 4–8.

in 2 Chronicles 20:5–12; Nehemiah's prayer in Nehemiah 1:5–11; and Paul's prayers in Ephesians 1:17–19 and Colossians 1:9–12.

Prayer Walks
(All ages)

Children are terrific prayer walkers because they enjoy movement, and being "on site" to pray makes prayer more meaningful and concrete. To begin, find a short route, like a prayer walk around your block to ask God's blessing and salvation on each family. Or prayer walk around your child's school. Look for visual cues like the disabled parking sign that can remind you to pray for all the handicapped students, or the stop sign at the crosswalk where you can pray for safety and protection for each child who attends school there.

When you stroll to the park, pray a blessing on each home; as you go, ask God to speak to you of what's on *his* heart for your neighbors. Or go to a hillside at night, where the lights of the city are visible, and ask that God would shed his light into your community where it's most needed.

Prayer Posture
(All ages)

The Bible talks of many ways in which people pray. It's important to give kids the freedom and variety of talking to God in different postures: sitting, standing, walking, kneeling, with hands raised, with clapping to show praise, bowing, or lying prostrate. When you have your next family prayer time, have each person pick a different posture in which to pray.

Journal Jots

For Your Child to Write About

Keep a Jehovah-Jireh Journal. Make a place in your journal to record God's provision in your lives (a friend, a good teacher, money for a mission trip or vacation). Since Jehovah-Jireh means "Lord, our Provider," write down the specific ways that God has provided something or answered prayers. Then when times seem bleak or you're discouraged, you have a place to go and be reminded of God's constant good care of your family.

Bookbag

Resources for Parents

Fuller, Cheri. *When Children Pray: How God Uses the Prayers of a Child.* Sisters, Ore.: Multnomah, 1998. All ages.

_____. *When Families Pray: 40 Devotions to Build, Strengthen and Bond.* Sisters, Ore.: Multnomah, 1999. All ages.

_____. *When Mothers Pray.* Sisters, Ore.: Multnomah, 1997. All ages.

Dobson, Shirley, and Pat Verbal. *My Family's Prayer Calendar.* Available for each new year in Christian bookstores or from Focus on the Family, 1-800-A-FAMILY.

Keffer, Lois, ed. *Hooray! Let's Pray! All Kinds of Prayers for Involving All Kinds of Kids!* Loveland, Colo.: Group, 1997.

Johnstone, Jill. *You Can Change the World.* 2 vols. Grand Rapids: Zondervan, 1997. An excellent guide on praying for unreached people groups around the world.

PrayKids! Adventures with Jesus in Prayer. NavPress. *Pray!* magazine's new magazine to encourage the prayer life of children. For ages 7–10. To order sample copies, call 1-800-366-7788 or go to www.praykids.com.

For research on the prayers of great men and women:

Bennett, William J. *Our Country's Founders: A Book of Advice for Young People.* New York: Simon and Schuster, 1998.

Elliott, Lawrence. *George Washington Carver: The Man Who Overcame.* Englewood Cliffs, N.J.: Prentice Hall, 1966.

Lockyer, Herbert. *All the Prayers of the Bible.* Grand Rapids: Zondervan, 1959.

Marshall, Catherine, ed. *The Prayers of Peter Marshall.* New York: McGraw Hill, 1954.

Use Prayer Tools
(Ages 18 months and up)

While all kids are wired by God differently, there's one common denominator: like little Energizer bunnies, they like to move! Capitalize on that by using prayer tools that encourage movement. You might use a plastic, blow-up globe you pass in a circle from child to child to pray for the world, prayer sticks (dowels with different colors of thin satin ribbon attached to the end) children can wave as they praise and pray, or prayer games like Musical Prayers (a prayer target is taped to each chair, and when the music stops, all the kids sit or kneel at their chairs and pray for that need).

part three

following God

Following God and his ways has always been a high priority in his kingdom. "I command you today to love the LORD your God, to walk in his ways, and to keep his commands ... then you will live and increase, and the LORD your God will bless you," he told his people long ago (Deut. 30:16). It wasn't the first time God asked to be followed, and it wasn't the last. He repeated the message throughout the pages of his book, the Bible.

God hasn't changed. He still wants his children to follow him and obey him—not because he is a killjoy but because he has a future and a hope for us and desires for us to live the most thrilling, fulfilling life possible—better than we could dream of for ourselves.

But you won't follow someone you don't know and enjoy. And you won't willingly follow someone you don't love and feel loved by.

With an enjoyment and love for God growing in your child's life, we now turn to the Following God section, which includes the Ownership Window, the Obedience Window, and the Church Window. As your child begins to know and love the Lord, he slowly begins to take more initiative for his relationship with God (the Ownership Window), and an obedience from the heart begins to be formed in him—not overnight but in graduated epiphanies, little by little, year by year (the Obedience Window). Yet God doesn't expect him to do it alone; he provides family and the community of faith, the local church, to support spiritual growth (the Church Window). Let's continue as we see what happens when a young person's faith grows from what Mom and Dad taught her to an "ownership" of her relationship with God.

Talking about God is like teaching kids to ride a bicycle. You put the training wheels on. Then you hold the kids on the bike as they start to pedal. Eventually you have to let them ride on their own.

—Lawrence Cunningham,
Reader's Digest

The day comes when your children must get off your shoes and be full partners with the Lord in a divine dance. The day comes when your children must stand before God's throne alone and declare solely by their own will that they have chosen the faith that has been chosen for them by their parents.

—Phil Phillips,
Helping Your Children Walk with God

Trust in the LORD with all your heart
and lean not on your own understanding;
in all your ways acknowledge him,
and he will make your paths straight.

—Proverbs 3:5–6

The power to reproduce godly offspring remains primarily with the parent who loves the Lord, knows and obeys his Word, and is committed to the depth of his heart to produce godly offspring.

—Dr. Bruce H. Wilkinson, *Experiencing Spiritual Breakthroughs: The Powerful Principle of the Three Chairs*

eight

the ownership window

One of the most memorable moments for Christian parents is their child's awakening to faith. There's no other experience that can match the moment when you get to witness or help your child in a prayer of commitment to Christ. The joy is no less when you discover that in the quiet of her own heart, she already has invited Jesus in.

What God wants, and what any clear-thinking Christian parent wants, is for children to come to the place where they "own" their relationship with God. Some children, of course, take the long route on their journey of faith and make their commitment to the Lord in their teenage years—or later. While this may be nerve-racking to the Christian parent, not every soul is on the hoped-for evangelical timetable of "accept the Lord in the preschool years, rededicate or get baptized in the teenage years, and serve the Lord for life thereafter."

We all know by experience that faith grows in starts and stops. Mountain peaks and lower-than-low valleys in spiritual progress are common. Times of questioning or reflecting, away from the confines of church involvement, are not only predictable but, for some, necessary. Eventually, through prayer and persistence, tears and talk, a high percentage of people who grow up in a Christian home do put down the stake which says, "I give up. I'm yours, Lord."

Helping your child own a strong faith in Jesus Christ begins first with you, the parent. You must recognize and embrace the journey each child is on and get comfortable with the fact that you are not in control of this process. If you do try to control it, you may be ensuring that your child gets to his destination the long way.

Start at the Start

Every spiritual journey has a beginning—when the heart opens up to God. And often that moment of opening one's heart and inviting Christ in happens to our kids when we least expect it.

Back when her children were young, my friend Cheri was busily running on autopilot, doing all the right things as a mom. Every day she fed her kids breakfast, then ushered them into the playroom while she picked up the house and did laundry; later she ran errands, put the kids down for their naps, cooked dinner, and then bathed the children. Finally, bedtime would approach—that time of day when she and Christy, her four-year-old daughter, had Talk Time before lights-out. Christy loved it because she got to choose any subject to talk about with her mom.

> Fight the good fight of the faith. Take hold of the eternal life to which you were called when you made your good confession in the presence of many witnesses.
>
> —1 TIMOTHY 6:12

One night, Christy asked why people do wrong things. Cheri wasn't really paying attention. She was tired from the day's tasks and activities, as usual, and thought, *I've got to get this kid to sleep before I fall asleep in the chair.* But for a few minutes, they discussed how being bad and doing wrong things is sin and how it hurts God. Then Cheri tried to quickly move the preschooler on to talking about mother-daughter trivial stuff, reading a story, saying a quick prayer, and then—lights-out.

Suddenly Christy said, "I have been bad and sinned, Mommy."

"Oh, honey, I know, and you can talk to Jesus about that when you're a big girl. Now let's pick out a story."

"I want to talk to Jesus about it *now* and tell him I'm sorry."

Cheri's mother-antennae went up as she thought, *She's far too young to be speaking of such spiritual matters. I think we need to wait until she understands all the ramifications of what this means.*

"Now let's read this story of the *Velveteen Rabbit*. I know you're gonna love it."

"Mom, I want to pray about this *right now!*" the four-year-old said.

At that point, God grabbed Cheri's attention and spoke to her heart, "This child wants to be mine. *Listen to her.*"

Cheri finally got it. Once she turned from her agenda and paid attention to what God and her daughter were saying, she finally recognized that Christy's heart was wide-open to the Savior—this was Christy's time! This was the spiritual birth date God had picked for her daughter, and it was his Spirit who had wooed her. It was the moment when Christy responded to Jesus' knocking on the door of her heart—and her mom had almost missed it. After a time of heart-to-heart sharing about what it means to be a Christian and how to follow Jesus, Christy prayed a simple prayer of confession and committed her young life to God.

This was the beginning of Christy's ownership journey.

Around the age of twelve, Christy started hearing dramatic testimonies of other Christian teens and how Christ had changed their lives. There was always a distinct line, a defining moment—before and after. Being four years old at the time of her conversion, she hardly had a checkered past to repent of. She hadn't spent years trying to fill the void with drugs or searching for peace like other kids talked of. At age four, Christy had understood that she was a sinner and that she needed to make things right with God and ask Jesus into her heart. But since she couldn't even remember what she'd prayed then or how she felt at the time, Satan planted a seed of doubt about her salvation. He tried to sabotage her relationship with Jesus. Confusion filled her heart—for a time.

> It is God who works in you to will and to act according to his good purpose.
>
> —PHILIPPIANS 2:13

After much worry, a lightbulb went off in Christy's head, and she knew she could fix this by simply making sure. She prayed another prayer of repentance—the sinner's prayer—apologizing to God for her sin and asking him to help her keep him number one in her life. In a very real sense, Christy was taking ownership of her faith by recognizing that she needed to make an informed and willful decision.

Christy's next faith step occurred during high school, when her parents wanted to move to a new church. Christy made the decision to stay with her youth group at her old church. The parents wisely relented, knowing that good Christian friends are sometimes hard to make. These two decisions helped solidify her faith.

Then in college, her faith was sealed. Christy was the planner type and had her life already mapped out. With dreams of fame and fortune, she wanted to use the artistic talent God gave her to build a career as a professional artist. So she picked a college, got a scholarship, and felt very confident. Then off she went to be a counselor at summer church camp. The focus of camp was on missionaries, and Christy began to realize what God was asking of her.

> Since, then, you have been raised with Christ, set your hearts on things above, where Christ is seated at the right hand of God.
>
> —COLOSSIANS 3:1

She resisted with all her might until the last day. In the huge, open-air service, the speaker gave the call to anyone who felt God had beckoned them to the mission field. Christy stood motionless until the assembly dismissed. She walked back to the cabin with her head down so no one would see her red, puffy eyes. Then right in her path, in the middle of a dirt road, she found a little booklet. She opened it and read the first line: "Paul, a servant of Jesus Christ, called to be an apostle . . ." She didn't read any further. The miracle of reading this specific verse from God's Word spoke something so personal to her, she knew the Spirit was speaking.

She ran back to the cabin and, on her knees, gave it all up. She told God that he'd had her soul, but now he could have her very life. Laying her plans and future at his feet, Christy told the Lord she would do whatever he asked and go wherever he directed. Then she returned home after camp and awaited instructions. She truly thought the phone would ring and she would be called away to Africa.

In three graduated epiphanies, Christy had done what I've heard ministers challenge people to do: "Give as much as you know about yourself to as much as you know about God."

She gave her heart to Christ because she knew she needed a Savior.

She rededicated her heart to Christ and stayed where God's love could reach her because she wanted her growth to be certain.

She gave her life to Christ because she wanted his best for her future.

Each epiphany built on the other, laying the foundation for a lifetime of following the Lord. Since then, God's work in Christy's life led her to college and to a faithful husband, with whom she is now raising two young children. She's comfortable that the mission field for her may not be in a foreign land but in her own hometown. It doesn't matter. God made Christy a promise and has proven to her time and time again that

> So then, just as you received Christ Jesus as Lord, continue to live in him, rooted and built up in him, strengthened in the faith as you were taught, and overflowing with thankfulness.
>
> —COLOSSIANS 2:6–7

he is faithful. Now she's teaching her two little ones about the God she loves and has learned to trust. She remembers God's promise at every fork in the road: "Trust in the LORD with all your heart and lean not on your own understanding; in all your ways acknowledge him, and he will make your paths straight" (Prov. 3:5–6).

Find the Equator

What is the parent's role in a child's faith development? There are two poles, and the correct answer is usually the equator. Let me explain.

Arnie's parents not only were in church every time the doors opened in their small South Carolina town but believed there were appearances to uphold as well. As long as their four children were under their roof, church attendance and "correct Christian behavior" were to be observed. If not, the woodshed, threats of God's wrath, and emotional distance were the consequences. Forget the Enjoying God and Loving God stages, Arnie's parents knew only one stage: Obeying God. The Bible was a rule book to be followed, and any deviation was met with swift punishment. Predictably, Arnie spent most of the sixties and seventies in a drug-induced stupor, never even considering that there was a God who could be enjoyed, loved, obeyed, and served.

> Don't let anyone look down on you because you are young, but set an example for the believers in speech, in life, in love, in faith and in purity.
>
> —1 TIMOTHY 4:12

Pam's family on the other side of the country—Portland, Oregon—occasionally went to a mainline church where truth was relative. God was in nature, but the nature of God wasn't in Jesus. It was in good works, social justice, and higher education. You lived faith by trying to be good and do good and through "tolerance" of everything. With no absolute truth, no need for a Savior, and no knowledge of possible divine intervention, Pam had no North Star to look to when life started throwing fastballs at her. Her brother died of a drug overdose, her sister became a lesbian, her first marriage failed, her college-aged sons indulged in the excesses of frat life and were both kicked out of school. With a bottle of pills in one hand and the phone in the other, she called a Christian she knew from work and said, "You act like life has meaning. I'll give you ten minutes to try to convince me it does."

Both Arnie and Pam eventually found their way to the God of the Bible and the Savior from Nazareth. They most assuredly took the long route.

While we should always give God the freedom to work in his sovereign way, and while these two stories ended far better than they began, I'm not convinced that God makes people go through hell before they find heaven or that some souls must first come close to death before they finally find life. Perhaps a fallen world, fallen parents, ignorance, and willful disconnection from God are reasons some souls must come to the edge of hell. But I believe that it is never God's intention for it to happen this way.

Naturally we don't want our children to get close to those fiery gates, because the flames will always cause a nasty scar. Can we prevent this from happening? Unfortunately, no. Even "perfect" parents have children who must be snatched away from the enemy at the last moment. This fact, however, shouldn't prevent us from doing the right things to help our children own their faith as they grow.

What are the "right things"?

Live and model enjoying God
Live and model loving God
Live and model following God
Live and model serving God

And within our model of following God is the essential element of helping our child recognize that their relationship with God is their relationship with God.

We can't make them enjoy God or accept Christ for them, because their heart's door only opens from the inside.

We can't make them love God or listen to Christ for them, because the Spirit speaks in unique ways to us all.

We can't obey Christ for them, because God has graciously given them a will of their own.

We can't give them—or let them borrow—our abundant life in Christ because this is gained only by finding our individual path to service for the kingdom. But there is a great chance that if we do help them discover how they can serve with their gifts, our children will want to love and follow God.

Owning Their Start with God

Whatever age your children are, they can learn to enjoy, love, and follow God if you help them to realize the marvelous grace and forgiveness he has lavished upon them through the sacrifice of his Son, Jesus. As in the story of Christy, when she realized she could

Until we all reach unity
in the faith and in the
knowledge of the Son
of God and become
mature, attaining to the
whole measure of the
fullness of Christ. Then
we will no longer be
infants, tossed back and
forth by the waves, and
blown here and there
by every wind of
teaching and by the
cunning and craftiness of
men in their deceitful
scheming. Instead,
speaking the truth in
love, we will in all things
grow up into him who is
the Head, that is, Christ.

—Ephesians 4:13–15

not fix the "bad things" disease, her mother helped her to realize that God had already cured the consequences of sin for her. This was the point where her journey started. You cannot enjoy a Savior if you don't think you need to be saved.

Some little children understand their need for salvation. But others don't truly get it until they've experienced a bit more of life. A close friend of mine has two boys. Both accepted Christ at an early age. Now that they're teenagers, one is walking with God; the other doesn't sense the need. Why is there a difference? After all, they were raised by the same parents in the same church and have read the same devotions. The difference is that the oldest recognized he was a sinner who needed a Savior and the youngest hasn't fully grasped all of the eternal ramifications of not following the Lord closely.

Notice that I haven't said one is a Christian and the other isn't. There's no way anyone can know this 100 percent; only God sees the heart. But because the youngest hasn't recognized his need for a Savior, there is no reason for him to enjoy, love, obey, and serve the Lord. Conversely, the oldest is doing all four as much as his teenage maturity allows.

A lifeguard friend in San Diego told me that the hardest drowners to save are those who don't think they're drowning. Until they come to the point where they give up and let their rescuer do his job, they'll usually do one of two things: (1) fight until they threaten to take the rescuer under or (2) think they can save themselves and swim to shore on their own, usually drowning in their own effort and pride.

Parents help their children enjoy, love, and obey God by giving them the full picture of their own sin and the full story of God's grace. Let me illustrate five ways you can do both.

- *Don't venerate Bible characters except Jesus.* From Adam to Noah, Jacob, Moses, David, Solomon, Peter, and Paul, our Bible heroes were all humans who most definitely weren't perfect. While children's Bible storybooks are well-written, wonderfully illustrated, and gorgeously packaged, very few do well in painting our spiritual superstars as imperfect people who needed God as much as we do. While you don't have to go into the David and Bathsheba story with a six-year-old, allowing your child to see the warts on these people will show them more about human nature than only mentioning the good things they did. How is God's grace shown? By the fact that these people made mistakes but didn't let their mistakes keep them from following God and doing big things for him.
- *Don't venerate other adults the child looks up to.* Grandparents, older siblings, aunts, uncles—whoever is close to your child can seem larger than life and may appear "perfect." In an appropriate way and at the appropriate time, talking about the total package or letting the significant adult talk about their human foibles won't burst your child's bubble. It will point to God's goodness, God's grace.
- *Encourage the other adult leaders your child admires to share their faith stories.* Sunday school teachers, youth leaders, even the lead pastor all need to be real people who have overcome real mistakes by the power of God. Invite them to your home and have them share their testimony.
- *Read and listen to the testimonies of those who have strayed far from God, only to realize how much they needed him.* I mentioned this in an earlier chapter, but testimony time at church is getting to be a thing of the past. If this is the case at your church, read books, bring people into your home, even watch some Christian TV or subscribe to *Guideposts* magazine, to allow

your child to hear the faith stories of those who talk about the effects of sin and the grace of God.

- *Search for examples of people "learning the hard way," whether they've come to their senses or not.* I know a couple who, when their kids hit the teen years, took them into a local juvenile institution to meet with other teens who had started the process of making a habit of poor choices. It doesn't take long in this type of controlled environment to see where a series of poor choices—or even one stupid choice—can lead. They are living illustrations of the consequences that poor choices yield.

Encouraging Epiphanies

Dan used to be a youth leader at a church outside of Seattle. He understands the importance of young people making small but significant steps in their walk with Christ. He told me about one young girl, named Jennifer, who was in his youth group for six years. Though she came from a stable and loving Christian home, she was the strong-willed type. By age thirteen, she had pretty much tuned out parental sermons, family devotions, and adult church. But because most of her friends were in youth group, she kept within earshot of the Lord.

At church camp, between Jennifer's eighth- and ninth-grade years, she listened to the testimony of about a half-dozen high schoolers. In their own words, they admitted their imperfections and their need for the Lord. Something clicked inside Jennifer's head. "If *they* weren't perfect, I guess I didn't have to be either." The next summer, at the high-school camp, she came forward to, as she admitted, "give my life to Christ for the first time." Two years later, after some ups and downs, she rededicated her life to Christ. Three years later, as a camp counselor for junior highers, she spent time with the camp's speaker and "realized I had a heart to reach girls who were struggling in their walk with God." Today, she's a full-time Youth for Christ leader, raising her own funds to disciple other women volunteers and teenagers.

From the outside, it seems her parents had nothing to do with all these epiphanies, but Jennifer admitted differently. "I know I wore them out in high school by constantly rolling my eyes and tuning them out, but they never nagged or forced me to go to youth group or camps. I'm sure they prayed for me a bunch, and they always found the money to get me to camp. I had to find the Lord on my own timetable and through my own discovery. I tested what they said all through high school, and I found something out: It was all true."

But she had to find it out for herself, one epiphany at a time.

Thomas's parents had to be a little more proactive. They played into his artistic, inquisitive nature by choosing one man in the Bible who was like him. When he was about eight, they decided that David would be the biblical character they would constantly refer to. To understand their unique son and to help him find his way with God, they first studied the life of David. His history, his ups and downs, his words—all served to help Thomas make his way, one epiphany at a time.

When Thomas got pushed around on his seventh-grade football team, the lesson was "Goliaths will fall when courage and God are on your side." When he started writing poems the next year, his mom read him some of David's psalms. Two years later, when he was caught stealing candy with his best friend at a local supermarket, Psalm 51 served to show him that true repentance pleases God and makes you clean. By high school, Thomas and David were best friends, soulmates.

Giving Thomas the appropriate thirst for a "Bible friend" helped him make the transition to Jesus too. Though David was a hero that was human enough to relate to, Jesus was a Savior real enough to trust.

Why is the Ownership Window so essential?

Kids—young or old—will not share a faith they've borrowed. If they own it, they will share it with others. Owning a genuine faith leads directly to the window of obeying and serving. Without this essential step, which the child himself must fully realize, they won't see the wisdom of obedience or the joy of serving.

Making the Most of the Ownership Window

Keep the Date
(All ages)

If your child trusts Christ at an early age, get a Bible and mark down the day and time next to John 1:12. Then tell your child that anytime he doubts that he is really a Christian, he is to go to this verse and believe the facts of what actually happened.

Throw a Party
(All ages)

Just as you celebrate your children's birthdays, go all out for their spiritual birthdays. Buy presents, make a cake, invite church friends over—make a big deal about it. That way they'll know they have a spiritual birthday and can point to it every year as a marker of when they first made the choice to become a Christian.

Give Them Permission
(All ages)

Romans 12:1–2 talks about presenting our bodies to God as a living sacrifice. Help your children see that this isn't just a one-time thing—that every day, week, month, and year we can make a new commitment to God. It's just like telling someone you love them. You don't say it just once, but you say it over and over again. Tell your kids, "It's okay to rededicate your life to the Lord as often as you think you need to."

Heart to Heart

Think It Over and Share with Your Child

Think about how faithful God was in your life to bring you to true ownership of your faith. Thank God for those who, maybe even unknown to you, were part of that cloud of witnesses not only cheering you on spiritually but also praying for you—even when you were far off.

Starting the Day with God
(Ages 7 and up)

If your child has a desire for Christ to live through her, starting each day with a prayer of surrender can be a practical way for her to intentionally put her life in God's hands. Something like, "Lord, I want to be at your disposal. Before the day crashes in, I want to take my everyday, ordinary life—my going-to-work or school, eating, sleeping, and walking-around life—and place it before you as an offering. Renew my mind. Change me from the inside out. Keep my focus on you. And help me to abide in you, because without you I can accomplish nothing. So Lord, think through me and fill me with your Spirit today." This prayer is based on Romans 12:1 (MESSAGE). Share how you begin the day in conversation with God and encourage your child to make her own prayer.

Raise the Bar
(All ages)

If your children have chosen to own their walk with God, make sure they're giving God room to do miracles. By encouraging a prayer life that is courageous and unafraid to ask for anything—large or small—God will mark their lives with miracles that will undeniably prove his

Journal Jots

For Your Child to Write About

- In a world in which people grapple for answers yet think that "all things are relative," we must be ready to give a reason for our stand. This begins with defining the meaning of truth. Write the definition of truth. Jot down some Scriptures that state what truth is. (Older children)

- Write Your Reasons. In your journal, write where you stand on one or more of the following topics: abortion, rock music, euthanasia, dating. Here are some things to consider as you write: What does God say about this topic in his Word? Is there an example in Scripture that supports my argument? How could I explain my stand to people who don't know God? (Teens) love and personal concern. Nothing helps you own the supernatural better than continually experiencing the supernatural.

Communicate the Meaning
(All ages)

If your child has accepted Christ, spend some time before the next Lord's Supper is celebrated in your church to help him better understand its meaning. Read some of the verses below from a paraphrased or contemporary children's Bible. Talk about how the bread and the wine symbolize what Jesus did for us on the cross (see Matt. 26:26–28; Luke 22:19–20; 1 Cor. 11:23–28) and what it means to your child. In this way, you can help your child own this celebration of the abundance Christ offers us, and he can enter into it, instead of its being a ritual he can't connect with.

Lights in the World
(Ages 2 and up)

For a family devotion one night, get two flashlights, one with batteries and the other without. Turn off the lights in the room and explain that our world is full of darkness. Then turn one of the flashlights on, explaining that it represents the light of Jesus. The only way others will see this light is if we let Christ live through us and are powered by his Spirit. Then turn it off and turn on the flashlight without a bat-

---

Bookworm

Resources for **C**hildren

McDowell, Josh, and Bob Hostetler. *Don't Check Your Brains at the Door.* Nashville: Word, 1992. For ages 15 and older.

Munger, Robert Boyd. *My Heart, Christ's Home.* Downers Grove, Ill.: Intervarsity Press, 1992. For all ages.

_____. *My Heart, Christ's Home: Retold for Children.* Downers Grove, Ill.: Intervarsity Press, 1997. For ages 4–11.

O'Conner, Joey. *Breaking the Comfort Zone and 49 Other Extremely Radical Ways to Live for God.* Grand Rapids: Revell, 1998. For ages 10 and up.

Rothenburg, Joan. *Yettle's Feathers.* New York: Hyperion Books for Children, 1995. For ages 4–8.

tery. Explain that that's what happens when we are disconnected from God—there's no light to shine. Read and talk about John 3:19, John 1, John 8:12 and Matthew 5:16.[1]

Growing by Doing
(All ages)

One of the best ways to help your child's faith grow is to give her opportunities to share Christ in actions and words. As a family, have an evangelistic holiday outreach where you invite your neighbors for a meal and share the Christmas story or show the Jesus film. Brainstorm together for ways to show God's love to others or check out the ideas in chapter 11, the Joy of Helping Window. Give your children, no matter what their ages, a chance to put faith into action.

Can't Wait to Date
(Ages 11–18)

After previewing the book, read *Getting Ready for the Guy/Girl Thing* with your young teen or *What Hollywood Won't Tell You about Sex, Love and Dating* with your older teen, both by Greg Johnson and Susie Shellenberger (Regal). This is a good way to begin a discussion on intimacy and right timing in relationships. Pray and ask God to give you helpful answers. Remember, if you don't know the answer to your teen's questions, search for the answers together. He will be glad for your openness and honesty.

Bookbag

Resources for Parents

Arrington, Lael F. *World Proofing Your Kids: Helping Moms Prepare Their Kids to Navigate Today's Turbulent Times.* Wheaton: Crossway, 1997.

Burkett, Larry. *Money Matters for Teens Workbook.* Chicago: Moody Press, 1998.

Colson, Charles. *Answers to Your Kids' Questions.* Wheaton: Tyndale House, 2000.

Geisler, Norman L. *Christian Ethics: Options and Issues.* Grand Rapids: Baker, 1989.

Zacharias, Ravi. *Jesus among Other Gods.* Nashville: Word, 2000.

Fashioning and molding the spiritual character of
your child is the most significant work you can do....
You must assume the responsibility for developing
your child's character, and with the Master
Designer's help, nurture it, inspire it, and polish
it until your child's character is everything
God intended it to be—Christlike and
beautiful "from the inside out."

—Kay Kuzma,
Building Your Child's Character from the Inside Out

Obedience is the key to every door.

—George MacDonald

I have loved you even as the Father has loved me.
Live within my love. When you obey me you
are living in my love, just as I obey my Father and
live in his love. I have told you this so that you
will be filled with my joy.

—John 15:9–11 LB

nine

the **obedience** window

It was the midsixties, and ten-year-old Gary Rutledge will never forget his day of reckoning. He had just been caught stealing fifty-cents worth of candy by the owner of a mom-and-pop grocery store. The police weren't called; his mom was. "When your dad gets home," she said, "he'll decide what to do with you." Waiting the six hours in his room on a sunny summer day for his father to arrive home and dole out punishment was the toughest thing he'd ever had to do.

When his dad walked in the door, his look of "serious business" caused Gary's heart to sink. His dad wasn't a mean or violent man, but he sometimes had a hair-trigger temper when his boys got out of hand.

"Son, let's go out back for a talk," he said. Gary inched his way out the back door, not taking his eyes off of his dad.

After Gary recounted in vivid detail what he'd done that day, his father looked away for a few moments, then looked back into his eyes.

"What would you rather have, a spanking or being grounded for a week?"

Young Gary looked up in surprise. Before his dad could change his mind he said, "I'll take the grounding."

"Okay, you're grounded for a week."

The pronouncement wasn't followed by a hug but by a look— and a slight "every boy does dumb things" smile. A bond was formed. Dad had been calm and fair. Dad could be trusted.

Seven years later, when Gary came home stoned, reeking of marijuana and acting starved, his dad didn't overreact. He waited until the next day to confront Gary. Under his dad's calm demeanor, Gary tried to lie his way out of it but eventually cracked and confessed his wrongdoing. In his midforties today, Gary smiles as he remembers the consequences. "I told him I wouldn't do it again. Though I could tell he didn't believe me, he also knew that I was basically a good kid who had made a dumb choice. I was let off with a warning—and a hug. He proved trustworthy—again—with my immaturity. From that point on, I can't remember ever letting him down."

> Children, obey your parents in the Lord, for this is right. "Honor your father and mother," which is the first commandment with promise: "that it may be well with you and you may live long on the earth."
>
> —EPHESIANS 6:1–2 nkjv

Parents want obedience from their children. Not an outward "I'll obey because I'll lose privileges or get punished if I get caught" obedience, but obedience from the heart. To a parent, obedience from the heart says, "I know that what I want to do isn't what my parents would want, and it's not good for me anyway, so I'll make the right choice and not do it." (Tuck that quote away, because I'm going to refer to this later, when I talk about what God wants from us.) Josh McDowell and others have said for decades: "Rules without relationship will yield rebellion."

Disobedience from children is inevitable; long-term rebellion is often preventable. Gary's dad proved himself trustworthy, so there were no consistent and destructive acts of rebellion. Instead, there was a heart attitude in Gary that wanted to please someone he loved—and someone who loved him. Gary's behavior wasn't always perfect; it couldn't be. But as he grew, Gary began to recognize his mistakes and tried to do better. No parents could want more from their child—and God could want no more from a follower.

This chapter isn't about how a parent can discipline to get obedience; it's about how children—and Christians—develop obedience from the heart and self-discipline due to an understanding of why obedience is an essential window to pass through before the Serving God Window can be peered into. Our hope as parents is that our child learns to obey without being coerced or punished. Likewise, it is God's goal that *his* children learn obedience without coercion or punishment.

God's Heart

Jesus said, "If you love me, obey my commandments" (John 14:15 NLT).

There it is. Simple and to the point. Love first, then obedience.

Enjoying God is the precursor to loving him. Loving God is the precursor to obeying (following) him. And in this chapter, we'll see that obeying God is the precursor to serving him.

Your goal as a parent is to show your children how worthy of trust, love, and obedience the invisible God truly is. It's a heavy-duty responsibility, because it means that most of the time, you must *act* like him. We talked about that in the Loving God chapter, but it bears repeating here because it's crucial to the obedience issue. As Emmett Cooper and Steve Wamberg write, "The biggest favor we can do for our children, or any others, is to love them the way Jesus loves them so they will decide to follow Him forever."[1] The reason for this is that kids often learn God's character and whether he's worthy of their love by how their parents behave toward them. The old "My dad abused me for years, so I could never fully come to God as Father because my father couldn't be trusted" axiom is not trite; it's true.

> And I delight to do your will, my God, for your law is written upon my heart!
>
> —PSALM 40:8 lb

The Why of Obedience

So why do you want your kids to obey?

Because, "you're the mommy!" (This is an okay answer when they're little but doesn't work well as they get older.)

Because you're bigger and know better. (True, but you're not quite there yet.)

Because as a wise, loving, and "been there" parent, you have a handle on what happens when certain rules aren't obeyed. (Bingo.)

You know what will happen if your two-year-old puts his hand on a hot woodstove. You know that a sharp object in the hand of a three-year-old is going to mean blood. You know that if your child doesn't look both ways when she crosses the street, the result could be life-altering for all concerned. You know that if your teenager has sex before marriage, there are a dozen or more consequences that could change his life. Experience and wisdom have convinced you that teaching your kids to obey your word will not only prevent lifetime scars from developing but will also improve their quality of living.

> Help me to prefer obedience to making money! Turn me away from wanting any other plan than yours.
>
> —PSALM 119:36–37 lb

Okay, parent, make the transition. Why does *God* want *you* to obey?

He wants obedience for the same deep-down reason a parent does—He knows what will happen when the rules aren't obeyed. And he loves you so much, he wants you to follow his wisdom so you can live the best, most fulfilling and productive life possible. He knows what an affair will do to a marriage so he says, "Let the marriage bed be kept pure" (Heb. 13:4). He knows that anger, if left to fester, will destroy once-close relationships, so he says, "Do not let the sun go down on your anger" (Eph. 4:26 NASB). He knows that if we are relentlessly riding our kids, they'll rebel, so he says, "Fathers, do not exasperate your children; instead, bring them up in the training and instruction of the Lord" (Eph. 6:4).

He knows. His heart for you is the same as your heart for your child, only a thousand times more loving and faithful.

Ask yourself, "Do I obey God out of fear or love? Do I fully grasp the love behind God's warnings and wisdom? Or do his commands seem unattainable and burdensome?"

As Christian adults, most of us don't disobey God out of ignorance. We know God's Word well enough to know compromise and flat-out disobedience when we do it. We know what he asks but don't always do it, do we? The truth is, we can't. That's why Paul laments his sin dilemma in Romans 7:20: "Now if I do what I do not want to do, it is no longer I who do it, but it is sin living in me that does it."

And that's also why as we encourage our children to obey God, we can't miss the most important element of all: Grace.

While we're challenged to obey Jesus because of our love for him, Paul says that ultimately we can't fully obey because of our sinful nature. If we were to get stuck in this dilemma, guess what would happen? We would never move on in our Christian life to the serving stage. We would never feel worthy of receiving his gifts and using them for his kingdom. Without the power of the grace of God, we would likely get so frustrated and depressed about our ability to live the Christian life that we'd leave it all behind.

Obedience and grace fit together like a hand in a glove. You can't teach one without the other. Exemplifying obedience to God without communicating a reliance upon God's grace portrays a law-oriented gospel that will obstruct your child's spiritual growth, making her unable to move on to serving God from the heart. Heart obedience develops only within the context of a firm grasp of the grace of God. Christians can obey God for a period of time without knowing true grace, but they will be unlikely to serve him if the grace of God can't be laid hold of. And parent, your children either learn or do not learn grace—from you. From your parenting style, your walk with God, and your teachings about obedience.

> And now a word to you parents. Don't keep on scolding and nagging your children, making them angry and resentful. Rather, bring them up with the loving discipline the Lord himself approves, with suggestions and godly advice.
>
> —EPHESIANS 6:4 lb

I've seen the statistics on how churchgoing students are leaving the Lord in droves, and I have to wonder if a lack of comprehension on the relationship between obedience and grace isn't one of the primary reasons. They hear about both, but they only understand obedience and how hard it is to obey. Further, since many haven't been shown how to enjoy and love the Lord before they've been told about obedience, they have, in essence, gotten the cart before the horse. So when they hear about obedience, they don't always understand the whys of it and God's true motive behind it. And then when they can't fully obey, they get discouraged and give up. It is, of course, natural that you'd walk away from someone you didn't truly love who told you to obey.

> If you stay in me and obey my commands, you may ask any request you like, and it will be granted.
>
> —JOHN 15:7 lb

A friend of mine wrote about an incident in which his young teenage son did something for which he deserved punishment but was instead rewarded with grace. "It was shaping up to be the best day of the year," he writes.

My 13-year-old's last day of middle school landed on a Tuesday, and it just so happens that the Seattle Mariners were playing an interleague game with the Colorado Rockies that night in Denver. We were able to get first-level tickets on the right field line the Sunday before. That meant he'd have great seats to see his favorite baseball player: Ken Griffey Jr. How favorite? A dozen posters, 100 baseball cards, pennants, cereal boxes, a street sign ... you get the picture.

So here we were: Last day of school, Junior, great weather, I get to leave work early, five hours with my son ... how could it get any better than this?

My day dragged in anticipation of getting on the freeway for the one-hour drive up to Denver. Then about 1:00 p.m., I got a phone call. My wife had heard that some of the eighth graders were planning to skip the last day. She called the school to see if our son was among them. He was. "Last night he asked for extra money for lunch. I didn't think about it at the time, but he knew he was going to skip," she said. I answered back, "And didn't he skip a few weeks ago, and you told him not to do it again?"

Sure enough, it was premeditated.

"Not only is he NOT going to the game," she concluded, "but he's going to be doing chores around here until there ain't no more."

I was speechless. Between some mild anger, I was hurt. Crushed is more the word. *How could he do this to me? To us? Didn't he realize there would be consequences? Why would he mess up all of our plans to skip the easiest school day of the year?*

My wife said something about trying to sell the $25 tickets to someone, but I couldn't. "I'd rather he had to rip them up in front of me," I barked. I could barely see straight, let alone think clearly.

You should know that my son and I have a very special relationship. He's a great kid. Our "easy" teenager (compared to his older brother). Loves the Lord, is a good friend, funny, compliant. We'd rather spend time with each other than almost anything else.

When he got home at 3:15, he called me at work. Amidst his predictable lame excuses ("last day," "all my friends were going," "we didn't do anything wrong"), I told him that actions have consequences. He started crying. Then I started crying. All the while, all I could think was, *How could he do this to me? To us? Yes, it was just harmless fun—and all of his lame excuses were accurate, but he deserved to be punished.*

We hung up. I shut my office door and looked out of the window. When I saw the mountain outside I began to think thoughts a little bigger than myself. Good thing it was a sunny day. "What would you do, God?" I said out loud. Immediately, my thoughts answered back (I'm a little too Baptist to say, "God spoke," but it was fairly close). *I cannot count the times I was looking forward to doing something special*

with you—for you—but you disobeyed. You followed your own path.
What you are feeling now is how I feel when we don't get to do some-
thing special together . . . when I want to bless you with a rich time,
but your actions often force me to withdraw the blessing.

"But there are times when I know I mess up, God, and you
do something that blesses me anyway," I answered back out
loud.

I cannot help but bless you. It is my nature to be full of grace.

As soon as I heard the word "grace" come into my head,
I knew what I needed to do. I must use this as an illustration
so that my son will get a clear picture of God's grace. *Some-*
thing given that is undeserved; unearned.

I dialed home to talk it through with my wife. (Just in case
I heard wrong.)

As badly as we both wanted—in our human hurt and
anger—to take this blessing away from him, we agreed that he
and I should go to the game to help him solidify a part of
God's character he'll need to take with him the rest of his life
(and to give him an example to follow with his children).

He was relieved and thankful. I was relieved and thankful!
(And it wasn't the fifty bucks, either!) Some days, discipline is
the right choice. But then there are other times when we get
to show . . . grace. That mysterious character quality of the
Father we experience ourselves on a daily basis. If we were
truly honest, we'd have to admit that we want (and get) God's
grace more than we want (and get) God's discipline. Good
thing, right?

The power to discipline or show grace—and the discernment to know when to do what—well, only God is perfect in
how it's done. I know for a fact there are times when I've disciplined when I should have shown grace, and shown grace
when I should have disciplined. And I know for a fact that
God is constantly giving me more grace than discipline.

How perfect was I in hearing God's voice and doing the
right thing on this day? We had an awesome time together.
We talked about this very lesson, and he learned that men

don't make excuses but rather take responsibility for their actions. Oh, and Griffey hit a double and two home runs! Grace is a good idea.[2]

This father's big-picture goal of obedience from the heart for his son was likely sealed by this one decision to impart grace to his son.

The Lifelong Outgrowth of Grace

God doesn't impart grace to us simply because it's easier than disciplining or withholding blessings; he does it because it is the most effective way of getting the right *behavior* out of us and building the right *character* into us. To be sure, the Father will "discipline those he loves" (Heb. 12:6), but we also know that "he does not treat us as our sins deserve" (Ps. 103:10).

God's order in the new kingdom is that grace produces a loving trust of his character, which will in turn produce obedience from the heart, which in turn produces character (behavior) that will benefit us—and his kingdom—for as long as he has us on the earth.

> How can a young man stay pure? By reading your Word and following its rules.
>
> —PSALM 119:9 1b

The Father's desire is to build people (followers) "after God's own heart," like King David was. David didn't have perfect behavior, wasn't always obedient, but his heart was bent in a "Godward" direction. When he lost his way, he could return to a God of grace who was always just a look inward and a glance upward away.

When our children are little, we *must* have their obedience to keep them from harming themselves. In fact, while "yielding to loving parental leadership, children are also learning to yield to the benevolent leadership of God himself."[3] But as they grow, we must slowly—but intentionally—transfer *obedience to us* to the heart decision of *obedience to God* through the realization and full comprehension of grace. By accomplishing this goal, we build their character and set them up to be lifelong servants of God.

Obedience and discipline aren't just for the purpose of getting our kids to exhibit behavior that makes us proud but to help them develop self-discipline. During childhood, there is a window of opportunity to lay the foundation for this fruit of the Spirit, and there is much we can do in our family lives to develop self-discipline in our kids, helping them to become more obedient to us and to their heavenly Father.

Making the Most of the Obedience Window

The goal, as stated earlier, is to move our children to the point of obedience to God (and us) from the heart. In practice, this is self-discipline. I have friends who have told me that all it took to make them obey was a parent's stern or loving look. Now, as adults, when faced with decisions of whether to obey God, they have transferred that example to imagining "the look" of God. Invariably, they don't picture God giving them a look of "make that decision and I'll withhold my blessing from you." Instead, it's a look of a loving parent that smiles, shakes his head with a knowing glance, and communicates "you *know* better, you *are* better, don't settle for second best."

The "eyes of the Lord" that search the earth and search our heart aren't trying to find those who are being "naughty and nice"; those eyes that serve as the North Star when we've lost our way are full of grace. "No, come this direction. You'll be glad you did." The habit of looking into those eyes must be built into our children.

Heart to Heart

Think It Over and Share with Your Child

Maybe there was a time that you failed to be honest or did things your way instead of God's way and experienced the hard consequences. Share the story with your child and talk about how disobedience affects our lives or how you experienced God's grace in your failure.

Play the "I Could Have" Game
(Ages 3 and up)

As adults, we make choices without thinking, based on the moral foundation we've chosen and have become accustomed to. How did you get to these automatic choices of self-discipline? Through practice, trial and error, and realizing costs and benefits. To teach discernment and self-discipline, help your child see that each decision comes with several choices.

"Did you see how Mom gave back the ten-dollar bill to the cashier when she overpaid me? I could have kept it, and no one would have known. But God would have known, and I didn't want to let him down."

"Did you see how I didn't yell at the teacher when she let you go outside in 30 degree weather without a coat on? I could have made my point in a different way, but I chose to handle it as a quick suggestion amidst other questions. That way the teacher didn't feel stupid or defensive."

The "I could have" game can be played with any child at any age. This activity will exemplify that they have choices every day between doing good or not-so-good and (hopefully) will show them the benefits of making right choices (obeying from the heart). It's an intentional way to lead a child to obedience from the heart, but the truth is, not all children are perceptive enough to catch it on their own. They need leading.

List the Choices
(Ages 5 and up)

Whenever you read Bible stories to your child individually or as a family, it often seems like the Bible character never makes the wrong choice. Teach them to think of other choices the person likely struggled with. "What could

Journal Jots

For Your Child to Write About

Pick one of the suggested Bible stories for learning about the benefits of obedience such as Noah, Abraham, Joshua and Caleb, and write in your journal what you learned.

Daniel have done instead of obeying his conscience?" "Why did Peter make the right choice and Judas make the wrong choice?" This allows your child to see that we humans go through a mental list of choices that can lead us in a variety of directions.

The Benefits of Obedience
(Ages 4 and up)

If you took thinking about choices to the next level, kids could learn even more. "What are the benefits and consequences of each choice?" Peter chose to accept Christ's forgiveness, Judas didn't. Peter lived, Judas killed himself. As you read Bible stories together, look for the value and benefits of being obedient to God and his ways. The stories of Noah, Samuel, and Esther are good places to start.

Self-discipline and a heart of obedience are developed by the example of your own life and that of the Bible characters your child should come to know.

Learning Obedience through the Power of God's Word (Ages 4 and up)

When Simon was becoming a cocky basketball player, saying things like, "I'm the best shooter; you're lucky to be on my team," and not sharing the ball with his team-

---

Bookworm

Resources for Children

Haidle, Helen. *Walking with Jesus One Step at a Time: Kids' Real-Life Stories.* Grand Rapids, Zondervan, 1999. A one-year devotional for ages 8–12.

Hunter, Emily. *A Child's First Steps to Virtues.* Eugene, Ore.: Harvest House, 1995. For ages 7–11.

McCallum, Jodi. *Good Manners and the Golden Rule.* Cincinnati: Standard, 1999. For ages 3 and up.

Silverthorn, Sandy. The Kirkland Street Kids series. Colorado Springs: Cook Communications, 2001. Includes *Gregory Is Grouchy, Sarah Is Scared! Bradley Is Caught* and other titles. For ages 4–7.

Thayer, William M. *Gaining Favor with God and Man.* Bulverde, Tex.: Mantle Ministries, 1989. For ages 13 and older.

mates, his parents had him memorize a Bible verse that addressed his attitude: "Take my yoke upon you and learn from me, for I am gentle and humble in heart ... For my yoke is easy and my burden is light" (Matt. 11:29–30). At first it didn't click, but then after several days of saying the verse from memory, Simon suddenly got it. He started giving the ball to other players and building them up, and he even enjoyed the game more. Help your kids learn and internalize God's Word, which will help them develop an obedience to his ways that will amaze you!

Going the Extra Mile
(Ages 6–12)

During the days of the Roman Empire, it was customary for a Roman soldier traveling on foot to call on a citizen to carry his bags. The legal requirement, however, was one mile. When Jesus told his followers to "go the extra mile" in the Sermon on the Mount (Matt. 5:41), he was encouraging them to fulfill more than just the legal obligation. He was asking them to exercise a form of love, no matter how hostile the authority. The next time your child is asked to do something by a parent, teacher, or other authority figure, help him think of a creative way to go the extra mile. If he's asked to feed the dog, he can clean out the dog's bowl

Resources for Parents

Campbell, Ross. *How to Really Love Your Child*. Wheaton: Victor, 1980.

_____. *Relational Parenting*. Chicago: Moody Press, 2000.

Cloud, Henry, and John Townsend. *Boundaries for Kids*. Grand Rapids: Zondervan, 1999.

Dobson, James. *Preparing for Adolescence*, updated edition. Ventura, Calif.: Regal, 2000.

Kuykendall, Carol. *Loving and Letting God*, revised edition. Grand Rapids: Zondervan, 2000.

Kuzma, Kay. *Building Your Child's Character from the Inside Out*. Colorado Springs: Cook Communications, 1988.

first. If she is asked to make her little brother's bed because he's ill, encourage her to pick up some toys or draw a picture to tape on the wall and cheer him up.

The Power of Your Example
(All ages)

Nowhere is your example more important than in teaching godly values and biblical principles. Your example is your most persuasive, powerful tool. So if you want your child to grow up honest, don't call in sick at the office when you're really burned out or want to play golf. If you want her to stay on the soccer team even though they've lost every game, let your daughter see you persevering on a difficult project at home or work. Share a bedtime story about a time you were tempted to throw in the towel but persevered, finished the job, and were blessed.

Clear Expectations and Affirmation
(All ages)

Sometimes kids don't know what parents expect. Use words and explanations that help you know that your child understands your expectations and rules. Then praise your child when he shows the behavior you desire and encourage him with hugs, affectionate pats, and loving words. When misbehavior occurs, let him know he is choosing to experience the consequences of his actions—and don't forget to follow through. If disciplining your children effectively is difficult for you, read *Boundaries for Kids* or *Relational Parenting* (see Bookbag: Resources for Parents for more information).

Like a Mustard Seed
(Ages 3–12)

God said that if we have faith in him, nothing is impossible for us—even growing more like Jesus! His Word also says, "Without faith it is impossible to please God" (Matt. 17:20; Heb. 11:6). Look at biblical role models of faith and obedience in God, like Noah in Genesis 6, Abraham in Genesis 12–24, or Caleb and Joshua in

Numbers 14. Then get some mustard seeds from a local nursery, farm co-op, or spice counter at the grocery store, and show your kids how small these seeds are. Talk about how our faith grows as we follow God and are obedient to him in our day-to-day lives.

If Jesus made time for the children and considered them His top priority … If Jesus admonished Peter *first* to care for the little ones … then we as parents must do our utmost to get our children involved in a church that follows Jesus' example and commands.

—Phil Phillips,
Helping Your Children Walk with God

If a church could accomplish only one thing with a child through his first five years of life, it should seek to help the child firmly sense that he is loved by the people at church. In this way a foundation is established to help the child see the church as more than a building, but as a group of people who love God and love each other.

—Wes Haystead,
Teaching Your Child about God

If you want to make room for God, you must make room for the children.

—David Walters,
Kids in Combat: Training Children and Youth to Be Powerful in God

I was glad when they said to me, "Let us go to the house of the LORD!"

—Psalm 122:1 NKJV

ten

the church window

I really *was* glad when Mom said, "It's time to go to church!" I still recall the way the hymnals and lemon-butter cookies smelled and how the bright red Kool-Aid tasted on warm summer mornings in vacation Bible school. I have fond memories of singing "Jesus Loves Me" and "What a Friend We Have in Jesus" in Sunday school, racing to find the Scripture verses first as we lined up for Sword Drills, playing the guitar and singing with my sisters at the mission in inner-city Dallas when I was eight years old and, later, bowling nights, choir, and church camps with the youth group. Somehow when we were all praying or singing together, I felt a little closer to God.

Ours wasn't a perfect church, but it was an anchor to me. I probably encountered a few grumpy Sunday school teachers along the way. But that body of Christians was a source of light to me, especially when my father died suddenly at the beginning of my sixth-grade year and things got shaky in my family. When we moved several months later, my new friend Mary's church provided stability in my life, even though I was the only one in our family attending it. Barbara, the youth director, loved and encouraged us awkward seventh and eighth graders. She was so full of joy, I wanted to be like her when I grew up. This continued to be my home church and was the place I chose to be married in following college.

These early memories of church are happy ones, filled with the joy of hymn singing, riveting tales of David the shepherd boy and Daniel in the lions' den, and the smiles of my teachers. While filing away countless Scripture verses in my memory bank, I also realized God loved me and responded by committing my life to him when I was twelve. Those memories were part of the reason I kept going to church even when I was struggling in my faith and why I later took my own children to church Sunday after Sunday. I wish all kids had positive memories of church, but unfortunately, they do not.

For some kids, church feels like rejection—a place that wounds or disillusions, closing their spiritual windows rather than ushering them into God's presence. Dan's parents took him to the local church—a rather rigid, rules-oriented place—until he was in the third grade. But then the minister died, and after the new pastor arrived, something happened that angered Dan's parents. Though he never knew why, they stopped going to church. In fact, ten years passed without Dan's parents taking their eight kids to church.

> Let the little children come to me, and do not hinder them, for the kingdom of God belongs to such as these.
>
> —LUKE 18:16

Dan missed being with other kids at church. When the family moved to a nearby farm, he began walking alone to a church in town where many of his school classmates attended—nearly three miles away. From middle school through high school, Dan never missed a church service or a Sunday school class. But instead of getting the love and acceptance he longed for, he got rejection. When Bibles were given to the sixth graders, Dan was left out. Only the kids whose parents were members got a new Bible. He wasn't invited for dinners in the homes of members, and the pastor rarely remembered his name. When Dan did go back to his parents' church (they eventually returned when the disliked pastor left) for a Sunday morning service, his mother leaned over to him at communion time and said, "You can't take communion; you're not a member."

As an adult, Dan drifted from church to church and finally joined one in the city where he lives. But he found himself easily angered at the other members. Sometimes he felt used when they asked him to cook and serve a dinner or contribute to the special building fund. When part of his contribution was left off a receipt, he got angry and didn't attend for a while. And now that the minister (whom Dan did like; the minister always spoke to him by name and appreciated his serving and help) is leaving, Dan's not sure he'll continue going to church. It's hard for him to feel God's love at church. He's still looking for acceptance from the people who call themselves Christians.

A Window of Opportunity

Entering into the Christian community through a local church is an essential part of any person's spiritual life, including children's. As Swiss psychiatrist Paul Tournier said, "There are two things we cannot do alone. One is be married. The other is to be a Christian."

> Dear friends, let us love one another, for love comes from God.
>
> —I JOHN 4:7

All our experiences in church are important, but this is especially so during the early years. Many of the attitudes people have about God, the church, and the Bible are developed during this time.

Another critical period is during the preteen years, when kids either become bored with church and Christianity or enthusiastic as they begin to serve God by serving others. Unfortunately, the attrition rate after middle school is alarming. More than half of all kids in the majority of denominations will leave the church during the teenage years, and many will never enter the door of the church again. Phil Phillips explains part of the reason for this:

> Disillusioned and alienated, our children leave the church. They look for spiritual nurture and power outside the church walls. And believe me, the world that the enemy has created offers a great many enticing "spiritual" and "powerful" alternatives to the genuine life-transforming power of almighty God. At the very heart of satanism and occult groups is the promise of spiritual experience and power—a counterfeit, to be sure, but also more experience and power than many of these children have been allowed

to or encouraged to experience in a church setting. And so, our children drift away in droves.[1]

The experiences our children have in church during their growing-up years are crucial. That's why we need to do all we can as parents to choose a healthy, vibrant church where our kids can grow spiritually and where children are a priority, then to be involved and do the things we *can* do to help church be a positive (not perfect) experience. While the only perfect church will be in heaven, we *can* find a place that aids and supports us in the job of spiritually parenting our children.

The church isn't the engine for spiritual growth; home and family are. But it's not the caboose, either. It can be a powerful ally in raising your kids to enjoy, love, follow, and serve God.

Sunday Hugs

Relationships with the people at church, especially leaders, have a great influence on how kids respond and how much they absorb and learn. In our co-authored book, *Extraordinary Kids,* Louise Tucker Jones tells how her toddler son Jay would run to their pastor after the worship service ended every Sunday morning. The pastor would scoop little Jay up in his arms and hold him while shaking hands with church members. Louise offered to take Jay, but the pastor refused. In doing this, not only did he show his own love for Jay, but he also allowed the church members to meet and love in a special way this child with Down's syndrome.[2]

> If one part suffers, every part suffers with it; if one part is honored, every part rejoices with it. Now you are the body of Christ, and each one of you is a part of it.
>
> —1 CORINTHIANS 12:26–27

Those Sunday hugs helped Jay to feel as if he "belonged" to the whole church. What a wonderful blessing that has been in his life. Now twenty-three years old, Jay loves Jesus with all his heart and looks forward to church. Surely that pastor's love helped nurture Jay's sweet spirit and set an example for the church body to follow. What if every pastor and church staff member modeled the same love and acceptance that Jay's pastor gave? Our churches would be a refuge for families with special needs who are seeking a place to worship.

What Can We Look for in a Church?

Recently, my friend Sandie told me how her grandchildren react when they pull into the parking lot at their Colorado Springs church. "Yeah! We're going to praise Jesus!" they say. These are kids who enjoy Jesus and love church because it's a joyous family event—not a "sit still, be quiet and bored" kind of service. They love the banners they get to wave during worship. Participating helps them feel involved. Then after praise and worship, they go to their own age-based classes to learn from God's Word.

> By this all men will know that you are my disciples, if you love one another.
>
> —JOHN 13:35

This points to a key consideration: Is your church a place where you and your children can experience God's presence? If they shout with glee when you pull into the parking lot of the church, it's a good sign!

Some other issues to consider when choosing a church are:[3]

- Is the children's and youth ministry a priority to the leadership? In other words, is the church investing in children and youth with loving leaders who are supported by the pastor and congregation? Are the children valued and respected? Does the pastor care enough to have the kids and their leaders up front on a regular basis to keep the congregation informed about what God is doing in these ministries and what the needs are?
- Does the church offer a strong Bible program to teach the children God's Word, to help them know God, to teach them how to pray and stand for their faith, instead of merely offering you a baby-sitting service?

- Are you as a parent going to be fed and ministered to by sound Bible teaching, so that you can be the spiritual leaders of your children? If not, you won't be as positive in your expression and support of the church.
- Are the children "made room for" or are they relegated to a second-class spiritual status until they grow up? Do they have opportunities to be equipped to minister and serve alongside adults, to learn to share their faith and be involved in an outreach program?
- If you're doing your part at home to nurture your child's faith, does this church seem to be one that will foster spiritual growth in your child?

I love what David Walters, author of *Kids in Combat,* describes as the church's most challenging mission: helping to develop children's spirits.

> This involves increasing their spiritual potential by teaching them how to know the Word of God and believe it. Trying to encourage or teach our kids to be merely good and moral is not enough. In these days we have to go beyond raising good kids . . . just being good is sometimes boring and no fun. God does not expect our youngsters to be good for the sake of being good. He expects them to be good to qualify them to become mighty. Too many children know the right answers but have a very limited relationship with the Supernatural God. Jesus did not pay the terrible price of dying on the cross to have a church full of bored, apathetic kids . . . but to raise up extraordinary kids.[4]

It's a high standard David holds up, but a worthy goal. And the church that puts kids *first* is greatly rewarded. In addition to raising up a flock of godly young people, the church itself is blessed. If you look around the nation, the most thriving, alive churches are those that give emphasis to loving and nurturing the faith of children. "An exuberance of these churches and an enthusiasm for the things of God are contagious. As a visiting minister, I can feel both the minute I walk in the door," says Phil Phillips.[5]

Making the Connection

Once you've found a good church, what can you do to help your kids connect? How can it be a positive experience? It all starts with your example. There it is—that role-modeling thing again! Your kids need to see your joy in going to church, not just observe your frustration at the effort it takes to make it out the door and get there on time. It helps to prepare the night before, by making sure clothes are laid out, and to have everyone up the next morning in time to eat and be ready. The night before, pray together as a family for your focus to be on God. Ask his Spirit to help you to know and love God more fully, to experience *him* at church, and that your worship may be pleasing to him.

You can also help your kids get connected at church if you:

> And let us consider how we may spur one another on toward love and good deeds. Let us not give up meeting together, as some are in the habit of doing, but let us encourage one another—and all the more as you see the Day approaching.
>
> —HEBREWS 10:24–25

- *Get involved.* When parents and kids have shared experiences, relationships are built. And church is no exception. It can be a source of some great conversations and can build bridges between you and your child if you teach Sunday school or work in the nursery or wherever your kids are from time to time. If you can't be the lead teacher, you could be a helper or substitute. You show how much you value them and their spiritual growth when you pitch in. Some of Holmes's and my favorite times in church were teaching junior-high Sunday school when Chris was in that age group, helping with the kids' Christmas drama when Alison was in the play, or hosting a high-school Bible study in our home. Ask God how he wants *you* to be involved with the children or youth.
- *Maximize the Sunday school experience.* When the teacher sends home worksheets, notes, or verses, read them with your

child. Help him with memory verses, ask good questions about how God spoke to him, what he liked best that day, or what he learned about God. Send the teacher a thank-you note sharing how God has worked in your child's life through the class or have her over for dinner so you and your child can get to know her better. The closer the relationship between teacher and student, the more he can learn and absorb.

• *Serve together.* Church shouldn't be a place where kids and parents are separated all the time. Doing things as a family at church, especially serving, can be a meaningful experience. On the Day of Kindness, when our church and other area churches combined forces to minister to people in a needy area of the city, parents brought their children to hand out bread and pray for people. Ministering as a family was a powerful experience for both the kids and the parents, but the community was also blessed by seeing families working together.

• *Get to know the pastor.* If your children or teens have sat down and talked with the pastor in your home during a meal and are developing a relationship with him, they are much more likely to tune in to his sermons. As a family, there are many ways you can be a blessing to your minister, such as praying for him and his family or writing notes of encouragement.

Keep a Balance

Church is great as a support and ally for your spiritual parenting. But avoid getting so overcommitted at church that you don't have any time at home. When you're at church so much that you have no time for prayer or family devotions, for fun, or for eating meals together, when you're always teaching other adults at church instead of teaching your own kids, it's a red flag!

As Mother Teresa said, "Love begins by taking care of the closest ones"—those under your own roof. Set some boundaries. Decide on one or two ways to serve or classes to attend and then "just say no" to the other opportunities. Or set a limit of only one night out

for church activities during the week so that there's time for home-work, reading, projects, and relationships.

"We want church to be a family experience for Jacob. We don't want it to always take us away from him and have to put him in the nursery," said one mom. So his parents have two commitments, the stewardship committee and involvement in the church's crisis pregnancy center. They involve their three-year-old son whenever they can. He sits with them in mass and goes with them to the walk-a-thon once a year.

When an older man sitting in front of Jacob and his parents during one church service scowled because Jacob asked a question, his dad asked the man if his son was disturbing him. "Yes!" he answered gruffly. They took Jacob out and later talked to their minister. He advised them to sit in a front row. They tried this and found that Jacob paid closer attention to the service there because he could see everything going on. Yes, he wiggles at times. But he also learns. His parents patiently explain the different parts of the service to him, and at home he plays church. They are amazed at the truths Jacob has learned in church and repeated to them later, when they had no idea he had been listening. How much he would have missed out on if they'd kept him in the nursery all those Sundays.

> Make every effort to keep the unity of the Spirit through the bond of peace. There is one body and one Spirit—just as you were called to one hope when you were called—one Lord, one faith, one baptism; one God and Father of all, who is over all and through all and in all.
>
> —Ephesians 4:3–6

Why keep a preschooler in the worship service? Matthew 18:5 gives one good reason, "Whoever welcomes a little child like this in my name welcomes me." Little children absorb more than you think. They begin to experience God through sacraments like the Lord's Supper, in Lenten and Christmas services, and by observing baptisms. They can pick up lots of information during that hour in the pew. You have to consider each child and his ability to sit through

your church services, but be sure to check out the suggestions in this chapter on preschoolers in the worship service.

When the Church Falls Short

You've found a church that you and your kids are excited about, start attending, and go along as happy church members. But then a year later there's a glitch. Instead of being the loving body God intends it to be, the church falls into disputes or the pastor messes up. What can we do when the imperfect group of people called the church falls short or fails completely? How can we keep our kids' spiritual life from being squelched or their faith disillusioned—how can we keep their heart open to the church when it's going through troubled waters?

When Jim and Sandy's church got a new pastor, he made sweeping changes and seemed to disregard the feelings of the congregation. When people didn't agree with his changes, he verbally ripped them apart. His abrasiveness hurt people, and they began to leave—in droves. Others criticized the pastor and gossiped. Sandy's son Chris, ten, was sad when he saw his friends leaving the church. Kids were asking, "Where are you going to go?"

> From him the whole body, joined and held together by every supporting ligament, grows and builds itself up in love, as each part does its work.
>
> —EPHESIANS 4:16

"What's going on, Mom and Dad? Why's our church torn apart?" Chris asked after church one Sunday.

Along with an explanation about what they felt were the problems, Sandy and Jim told their son, "We're not going to retreat, but we're also not going to gossip or backbite. We're going to seek God about what he wants us to do. Men mess up because they're men. If we put our full trust in *God,* not people, he will see us through. No matter where we are, God will be with us."

Because Chris's parents kept communication open with him about the problems and continued to seek God in the transition,

Chris learned at an early age some important lessons about keeping his eyes on Jesus.

When church embroilments or problems occur, we need to remember that it's not only the adults that hurt; children are affected too. We need to help them deal with their feelings (if their friends have left, for instance) and explain what we can about the situation without dumping too much information on them. They'll be watching our example, so it's wise to avoid even the appearance of evil—an opportune time to ask, "What would Jesus do?" and to keep up our family worship and devotion times at home so we don't become unplugged from God just because the church is in turmoil or because we're looking for a new one.

As we carefully select a church where not only we adults but our children and teens can thrive and grow in their relationship with God, help them connect with the community of faith by getting involved without being overcommited, serve and worship together, and help keep our children's spiritual life from being squelched when the church goes through problems, the church will become a meaningful part of their Christian life.

Making the Most of the Church Window

Role-Playing Church
(Ages 3–8)

Play church by letting each of your kids volunteer for a position: pastor, music leader, ushers who take up the offering, and so forth, and then role-play the service. Then change roles and let a different child preach or lead music. Use stuffed animals for the congregation.

I'm Bored!
(Ages 10–18)

What can you do when your child or teen says, "I'm bored! I'm tired of church" or "I don't want to go"? If kids aren't forced to go to church but go because that's what the family does every week, it doesn't have to produce a battle. Explain to your child the reasons you go to church and how you desire for her to develop a secure faith in Christ. Continue having family devotions at home, modeling your faith before her, and endeavoring to apply God's Word to your teen's everyday life. If he questions Christianity or challenges the beliefs presented at church, don't panic. Almost everyone goes through a crisis of belief where she reevaluates what she's been told and what *she* truly believes. Keep the lines of communication open and encourage her to continue to attend church with you even when she's not feeling especially close to God. In the meantime, pray up a storm!

Heart to Heart

Think It Over and Share with Your Child

- The church body is an important part of the believer's life. It can help or hinder spiritual growth. Think about experiences you had at church as a child and throughout your life—both positive and negative. Thank God for the good memories and ask him to heal the effects of the negative experiences you had at church.

- Talk to your children or teens about what they like most (and least) about church. Encourage them to share their earliest or favorite memories of church.

- Remember that your kids will tend to catch the enthusiasm for and be most influenced by the things that are a priority to you. If you drop them off at church and then go have breakfast, bow out of worship service to watch football games (ouch!) or coach soccer on Sunday mornings, they won't think it's important. What kind of nonverbal message about church do you want your kids to get from your example?

Pray for Your Children's Classes and Teachers
(All ages)

Pray that each of your children will get the most from their Sunday school and worship service experiences. Pray for a strong, vital youth group and children's program for your church. Pray for the children's pastor and youth minister! Pray that your child will have a desire to know God and his Word. If you haven't yet found a church that is a good fit for your whole family, pray that God will lead you to just the right place he wants you to be and that he'll show you how to be involved.

Opening Hearts
(All ages)

Of the children who attend church, those who have been ministered to by parents and have learned by watching their parents worship at home are much more likely to develop a hunger for God's presence and Word. Their hearts are more open and receptive to spiritual things. Spending time praying over your little ones, singing worship songs to them, playing worship or praise tapes, and reading the Bible to them regularly is valuable even if they don't seem to understand the parables or concepts.[6]

Prepare the Way
(Ages 3–12)

When your children are young, they don't have any idea of what's about to happen in the worship services. So go

---

Journal Jots

For Your Child to Write About

Read and discuss 1 Corinthians 14. Write down the names of several church members. Next to their names, write the ways that these members contribute to your church body and to the body of Christ. Example: Mrs. Schwartz—Coordinates activities for the youth group, plays the guitar; Mr. Benter—Visits the sick, helped me out when I had a problem getting along with a classmate. Then thank God for them.

through the order of the service with them. When Karen, a pastor's wife, did this with her girls, she acted the different ministry roles and showed them the different parts of the service. She explained the meaning and significance of the Apostles' Creed, the prayers of the people, the benediction. She suggested when they were to stand or sit, when they could read their Bible, look at their Sunday school papers, or fill in the blanks on the kids' sermon outline—after all, Dad was the pastor, and he loved it when they could tell him his three main points. Understanding the service helped them be more engaged when they were young. Now as preteens, the girls sing in the adult choir, light the candles, and shake hands with people after the service along with their father.

Happy Birthday (All ages)

Find out the birthdays of the pastor or the church staff members that particularly serve your children or family. Together with your child, send them a birthday card, thanking them for giving of themselves to the church family.

Bookworm

Resources for Children

Breckenridge, Marilyn S. *Jesse Tree Devotions.* Minneapolis: Augsburg/Fortress, 1985. Each devotion explains a Christian symbol of Advent and contains activities for families, with Scriptures and prayers. For all ages.

Burkett, Larry. *A Different Kind of Story.* Chicago: Moody Press, 1999. Check out all of Larry Burkett's Great Smokey Mountains storybook series. For ages 5–10.

James, Darcy. *Let's Make a Jesse Tree.* Nashville: Abingdon Press, 1987. Twenty-six different Christian symbols to make and learn about. For ages 5–10.

Make It—Bake It Stained Glass Suncatchers. Quincraft Corporation. Includes Noah's ark, angel, praying hands, etc. Available at Christian bookstores. For ages 5–10.

Water, Mark. *Children's Encyclopedia of Bible Times.* Grand Rapids: Zondervan, 1995. Kids can learn about the synagogue and what church was like for Jesus. For ages 7–12.

Get Your Teens Involved
(Ages 12–18)

Encourage your junior high and high schoolers to be involved in a vibrant, alive youth ministry. Sometimes during the teen years, kids can best hear and respond to truth through other godly adults. Being involved with their peers in prayer, outreaches or mission trips, Bible studies, or Christian youth camps can help them grow spiritually in the critical adolescent years. Parachurch ministries like Young Life, Fellowship of Christian Athletes, and Youth for Christ can boost their desire to know God and also to fellowship with other believers.

Faithful in Little Things
(Ages 2 and up)

No matter what his age, your child can be an active member of his church, serving even in small ways. He could dust the pews, help plant flowers around the church, organize the music library, clean communion cups, or pick up leftover bulletins after the service.

Love One Another
(All ages)

As a practical way of showing Christ's love, encourage your child to include new kids, disabled children, and others who aren't in her circle of friends at church, to welcome them with open arms rather than exclude them. This is the family of God, not a clique. One of the terrific things about church is the opportunity to have a different circle

Bookbag

Resources for Parents

American Tract Society. To order tracts or receive a free catalog or samples, call 1-800-54-TRACT.

Dilasser, Maurice. *The Symbols of the Church*. Collegeville, Minn.: Liturgical Press, 2000. Helps parents understand and explain the symbols of the church.

Family Friendly Ideas Your Church Can Do. Loveland, Colo.: Group, 1998.

Klein, Patricia. *Worship without Words: The Signs and Symbols of Our Faith*. Orleans, Mass.: Paraclete, 2000. Helps parents understand and explain the symbols of the church.

of friends than you have at school. Invite your child's Sunday school class over for pizza night so they can get to know each other better.

Sermon Research
(Ages 12 and up)

If your child has a special knack for details, he can offer his assistance as a researcher. Many times a pastor would like to enrich his sermon with details that he just does not have the time to find. Encourage your older children and teens to take notes during church and see if they can discover the three (or more) main points the pastor makes during the sermon.

Build a Bridge
(For parents)

Encourage your church to build a bridge to families with special needs and affirm the worth of their children by offering sign language for the hearing impaired, offering extended care for children with special needs during the worship service, or providing an aide in the classroom so that a disabled child can be included in Sunday school, choir, and other activities. By offering a place for all kids to be loved, cared for, and taught about Jesus, the whole body of Christ is blessed. For many other ideas on how churches can reach out to these special families, purchase *Extraordinary Kids: Nurturing and Championing Your Child with Special Needs* (Focus on the Family/Tyndale House) for your church library.

part four

serving God

When we enjoy God, receive God's love for us and begin to love him back, when we begin to focus on following God, a natural progression happens: we begin to see opportunities to serve God by helping those around us. We serve not for the purpose of doing good works to earn God's acceptance or assure our place in heaven but as a part of a normal Christian life, as an expression of our gratefulness for God's amazing grace and so others will know his love as well, and because serving him by ministering to others is what naturally is left in our wake as we follow him.

In John 13 when Jesus set aside his robe, girded himself with a towel, and began to wash the dirty feet of his disciples at their final gathering, called the Last Supper, he powerfully demonstrated the importance of serving God and encouraged them—and us—to do the same. "I've laid down a pattern for you," he explained (John 13:15 MESSAGE). "I gave you an example that you also should do as I did to you" (John 13:15 NASB).

It's very easy in our culture to focus on raising our kids to be happy, healthy, successful, churchgoing, good kids who make good grades and don't get into trouble. But there's much more to spiritual parenting than that.

"We seem to have forgotten that our children have been loaned to us as a gift from the Lord," says Dr. Bruce Wilkinson, "that our purpose is not to use Christianity to give them a safe and secure life, but to spend our opportunity as parents to raise them up as godly, committed, and wholly usable servants for God's greater purposes."[1]

Helping our children to experience what it means to serve God, to discover the joy of helping, and to discover the specific gifts through which God has equipped them to serve the body of Christ is a vital part of their spiritual development and an important aspect of passing on our spiritual heritage. It happens step by step, from the early years until they're grown. We will look at the Joy of Helping Window, the Spiritual Gifts Window, and the Heritage Window.

Children are God's apostles, day by day sent
forth to preach of love, and hope, and peace.

—James Russell Lowell, American poet

Do not let anyone look down on you because you are
young, but be an example for the believers, in your
speech, your conduct, your love, faith, and purity.

—1 Timothy 4:12 TEV

A church that doesn't provide youth with genuine
opportunities to worship and serve alongside adults
will watch its youth drift away. They won't see how
they fit into the bigger church.

—Miles McPherson,
The Power of Believing in Your Child

eleven

the joy of helping
window

When killer tornadoes ripped across Oklahoma in 1999, lives were lost and thousands of homes were damaged. The next night at bedtime, Elizabeth, John, and their three-year-old son, Jeremy, prayed for the families who had lost loved ones and for the boys and girls who had lost their homes, toys, pets, and personal belongings. Then Jeremy matter-of-factly stated, "I am going to build the people a house." That night he asked God to give him a real hammer, nails, and wood. His willingness to give struck a chord in his parents and made them wonder if they were doing all they could to nurture and encourage his heart to help. He may have been little, but his heart was big.

What makes children willing to serve and give to others? An open heart, some guidance, and the example of parents and teachers are the beginning. In Jeremy's case, although he wasn't yet big enough to build houses for people, his mom and dad helped him gather some of his good toys to give to children who had lost theirs. As a family, they went to the store to purchase flashlights, diapers, food, and other materials that were needed by victims of the tornadoes and delivered them to the church that distributed them to the families.

In this way, Jeremy got to experience the joy of helping others. But it wasn't the first time they'd reached out to serve or help others.

The family had built a foundation of compassion from his earliest years. From the time he was a toddler, he and his mom regularly baked cookies for a prison ministry that shares the love of Christ to those who are incarcerated. As they baked the chocolate-chip cookies, they prayed for the individuals who would eat them. They also kept a bank in the center of the dinner table to help feed needy children and to contribute to their church's effort to provide for homeless people in their community.

How Should We Live?

Giving your child a chance to experience the joy of being used by God to bless someone else is wonderful, but it's not the most important reason to serve and help others. There's an overriding reason we need to consider. In Ephesians 2:8–10 Paul tells us that we aren't saved by our works but by *grace;* salvation is a gift of God, not a result of our works. Yet "we are His workmanship, created in Christ Jesus for good works, which God prepared beforehand that we should walk in them" (NKJV). That means God has prepared or thought of these good works in heaven and he is looking for willing hands and hearts to carry them out on earth. As the Message renders that verse, "He creates each of us by Christ Jesus to join him in the work he does, the good work he has gotten ready for us to do, work we had better be doing." It's a mandate for Christians, not an option. We are to be rich in good works (1 Tim. 6:18), bear fruit in every good work (Col. 1:10), and work together *with God* (2 Cor. 6:1), colaboring for the advance of Christ's kingdom on earth.

> For we are God's workmanship, created in Christ Jesus to do good works, which God prepared in advance for us to do.
>
> —EPHESIANS 2:10

When you stop giving, you stop growing. Christians stagnate (even young ones) when they cease to become a conduit and become a bucket. We're designed by God to have him live his life through us. His nature is giving. So without giving, we cannot truly become Christ-like; we can't appropriate his full nature. Also, by giving, we show the world God's true nature. If all we do is intake, how can those around us truly know God's character? Serving is also about having enough of God's character and power to live the way he would live (serving and loving others and doing good works) and to let that attribute draw others to him— which it invariably will.

What might some of these good works consist of? According to Charles Colson in his excellent book *How Now Shall We Live?* Jesus' command to love our neighbors and enlarge God's kingdom means dispensing mercy and compassion to the destitute in mission shelters and soup kitchens, ministering to those in prisons and nursing homes, doing good and helping to create a new world of peace, love, and forgiveness in our own sphere of influence.[2] "When God makes us new creations, we are meant to help create a new world around us," Colson says.[3]

Children who are believers—even those at a young age—are not exempt from being meant to advance God's kingdom or to create a new world in our neighborhoods or circles. Kids can readily catch the idea that serving God means serving people if parents are demonstrating a lifestyle of giving. "Following and serving God means giving of myself, giving my time, my energy, my spiritual insight, my whole being to someone else, not because I have to but because I want to," says Adelina, a mother of three. She weaves this concept of giving to others into her children's everyday lives.

For example, she encouraged Charlotte, her three-year-old daughter, to paint a picture for an uncle who was going through a difficult time. After Charlotte painted the picture, they delivered it to him. Mom and daughter also send prayer notes to family and

> Command them to do good, to be rich in good deeds, and to be generous and willing to share. In this way they will lay up treasure for themselves as a firm foundation for the coming age, so that they may take hold of the life that is truly life.
>
> —I TIMOTHY 6:18–19

friends, letting them know that someone cares and is praying for them. Often the notes are sent unsigned and include a bookmark or flower. Many of the things they do are small, but Charlotte is being taught to care about people. Their lives are little pencils in God's hand, sending messages of his love to people in the world around them.

While young children are basically self-absorbed (one of their earliest words is "mine!" and they see life from one point of view—their own!), even toddlers and preschoolers begin to feel empathy for others who are sad or hurt. The more their emotional cups are full of love from parents and others around them, the more they are able to love others. Because it is normal early childhood behavior for children to be concerned about themselves, an attitude of service and giving is best learned by example.

Devon and John have involved their daughters in all that they do as they pastor and serve in the community. From the time the girls were very young, the parents let them help with small tasks of service. They often took them along on hospital visits and encouraged them to draw pictures for the people they were visiting. When Chelsea was five, she and her dad visited Margo, a lady dying of cancer, and Chelsea took her a picture she'd created. When John went to the home two days later, after the lady's death, he found Chelsea's picture tacked right by Margo's bedside.

When Chelsea and her sister Jessica were old enough, they babysat the children who came to a funeral, just to help out the family. But their greatest area of service has been at the nursing home. Wherever they live, they

> For I was hungry and you gave me something to eat, I was thirsty and you gave me something to drink, I was a stranger and you invited me in, I needed clothes and you clothed me, I was sick and you looked after me, I was in prison and you came to visit me.... Truly I say to you, to the extent that you did it to one of these brothers of Mine, even the least of them, you did it to Me.
>
> —MATTHEW 25:35–36 (niv), 40 (nasb)

go as a family once a month to the local nursing home. John shares a message of hope from the Bible, and Devon plays the piano. The girls gradually began to feel comfortable enough to shake hands with the elderly people and play their instruments for the residents. Once, the family made up care baskets filled with soap, shampoo, toothpaste, hand lotion, and other things for the residents who belong to their church. No holiday or special occasion, just an "I love you" gift.

While at first the girls thought it was a bother to go to the nursing home, they grew to love and enjoy going there and singing with their dad. They began to see the residents as people in need of friendship and love, not just as old people cast away by society. The girls were never forced but were given ongoing opportunities and the example of their parent's Christian compassion for a neglected group of people, and they soon got involved and found joy in using their talents to bless the residents.

> So my son, throw yourself into this work for Christ. Pass on what you heard.... Concentrate on doing your best for God, work you won't be ashamed of, laying out the truth plain and simple.
>
> —2 TIMOTHY 2:1, 15 message

Energized for Service

During the elementary years, from approximately six to eleven, children are in the process of developing a sense of industry and competence. They have a natural desire in this stage to be useful, to be productive, and to take on challenges. Giving them opportunities to serve others gives them a chance to develop new skills. As they try out different ministries, they discover what they do best.

Another important time to provide opportunities to serve is during the preteen years. This is the stage where kids either become bored with or excited about their Christianity. Often the church's focus during this stage is on entertaining them or having them memorize more verses. Memory work is great, but we mustn't leave out serving others, because as preteens minister to others, the theoretical becomes heart knowledge of God's Word, character is built, and the contagious joy of using their gifts to help others is experienced. As they step out in challenges, they realize that God can energize them to accomplish many things, can achieve his purpose through them, and can, in fact, do more than we could ask or think (Eph. 3:20–21).

During the teen years, children desire to make a difference, long to discover personal interests, and find direction for the future. If you open windows of opportunity for service and provide some gentle encouragement, you will see your teens take on responsibility in what they believe to be a worthy cause.

> And a little child shall lead them.
>
> —ISAIAH 11:6 rsv

Instead of raising up a group of bored, apathetic kids in his church, Pete Hohmann, children's pastor of Mechanicsville Christian Center in Virginia, has created teams, called Bridge Builders, who do outreach on a regular basis. After a Bridge Builders Boot Camp each summer, where he trains and equips them, Pete and the kids fly off for an outreach mission to share the hope of the Gospel, pray for people, and help in practical ways.

Each year the children prepare a musical, which they perform in inner-city Chicago, San Francisco, or wherever they're going to minister. Last summer, one of the twelve-year-olds, Mary, came to Pete and told him that she hated the musical they'd chosen and needed to leave the rehearsal because her heart wasn't right. Performing in front of people was also way out of her comfort zone, she added. He gave her permission to hate the musical and told her that not liking something doesn't necessarily mean you have a bad attitude. If she did her best to please Jesus even though she didn't like the musical, that would bring joy to his heart.

Later, Mary expressed what happened when she left her comfort zone and did her part to serve in the outreach: "The best thing I learned this summer was that it's not about me. It's about God and what he wants me to do, not what I want to do. There were things I really didn't want to do, but I did it anyway and made a sacrifice. And God came through and was so faithful!"

Henry Blackaby stresses in his book *Experiencing God* the concept of "spiritual markers" in our lives. A spiritual marker might be a great challenge that causes a crisis of belief. But as a child chooses to believe God's promises and to obey, God proves himself faithful. Thus the child comes to know God through personal experience and can look back to that spiritual marker in times of future challenge. Experiencing what it was like for God to use her and the team to touch others' lives was a significant spiritual marker in Mary's life.

Niki, twelve, another girl on the outreach, was fearful about sharing Jesus with people. "Before I came on Bridge Builders I was really shy. I didn't know if I could witness to anyone. I asked God to give me a boldness to pray and talk with people. Then I just felt a breeze blow, and I knew it was God. The next day I wasn't afraid to pray for anyone." Many times we try to protect children from "uncomfortable" situations, such as Niki's fear of witnessing and praying for others or Mary's dislike of the musical. But when we do, they miss a window to experience God for themselves. When Niki stepped out and served with the team, a spiritual marker was created in her life. She can look back to her first summer outreach and remember the faithfulness of God, which she experienced firsthand.

Making a Difference, Doing Good Works

It doesn't take a grand act of kindness or huge amounts of time to make an impact. And although taking kids on mission trips can be a powerful experience, you don't have to go out of town to help them make a difference. There are lots of ways to give kids an opportunity to serve. A seventh-grade group at Concord United Methodist Church in Knoxville, Tennessee, surprised everyone in their congregation one Sunday by washing car windows in the church parking lots. As people went out to their cars after church, they found the teens' labor of love in their sparkling-clean car windows. Visitors were

> He who is kind to the poor lends to the LORD, and he will reward him for what he has done.
>
> —PROVERBS 19:17

especially blessed and wanted to come back; hearts were touched by the kids' kindness.

Charles Colson tells of a fourth-grade teacher, Barbara Vogel, who taught her students about the Christian men and women in Sudan being sold into slavery. The children decided to do something about it and started a group called STOP. By saving their allowances and selling T-shirts and old toys, they raised enough money to free 150 slaves. Then the fourth graders wrote hundreds of letters to newspapers and lawmakers and raised over $50,000, which set over 5,000 slaves free.[4]

At Trinity Church in Omaha, Nebraska, a mom started Grand Friends ministry ten years ago. Debbie took the youth of her church along to a nursing home she frequently visited to model Jesus' love to the residents. Her purpose was to guide and challenge the youth to be Jesus to these people whom he loves so deeply.

Debbie and her teenage Grand Friends chose a neglected nursing home; each teen was then paired with a nursing-home resident and committed to write to that resident and visit them thirty minutes once a month. She coaches the teens in how to ask questions to discover the residents' interests and encourages them to play checkers or cards. In the process, the teens find that a little bit of their love goes a long way. The joy they experience by helping the seniors is more than worth the time they spend.

Whether it is the wheelchair-bound man who came home to Christ as a result of the love and prayers of one of the teens or the old man who hadn't talked to anyone in months but opened up and found hope through the love of another, the Grand Friends are making an eternal difference in the lives of elderly people in their community.

> You are the light of the world. A city that is set on a hill cannot be hidden. Nor do they light a lamp and put it under a basket, but on a lampstand, and it gives light to all who are in the house. Let your light so shine before men, that they may see your good works and glorify your Father in heaven.
>
> —MATTHEW 5:14–16 nkjv

When we give children opportunities to see us serving and involved in giving, it can influence the course of their lives. Diana, a missionary, told me how every Christmas during her childhood, her parents would invite an orphan from a nearby children's home to spend Christmas Day with their family and share fully in their Christmas celebration—the reading of the Christmas story, the stockings, the holiday meal, and receiving gifts just as the family did. They made an indelible impression on the orphans, and Diana and her sister learned how important it is to serve those less fortunate.

> By this all will know you are My disciples, if you have love for one another.
>
> —JOHN 13:35 nkjv

After Diana got married, she and her husband and three children ran a children's home for nine years and have served as missionaries. Diana's daughter now reaches out to the needy through her church. The pattern of serving and helping others was passed on from generation to generation, beginning with one kind act each Christmas season.

When kids learn compassion, they are learning to follow Jesus.[5] When you help initiate child-size or teen-size serving projects or give support to your children's ideas for how to help people, it gives them an opportunity to experience God's pleasure and to extend his kingdom on earth. Because they are really serving *him,* whether they minister to shut-in neighbors, prisoners, slaves, or abused children across the world. Kids can do the good works God has prepared beforehand for them to do; they can shine his light in effective ways. They can start small when they're young and will find out that as they rely on God, ordinary kids can change the world.

Making the Most of the Joy of Helping Window

Who Is My Neighbor?
(All ages)

Do you know your neighbors? With your children, make and take a covered plate of homemade cookies to a neighbor you have not

Think It Over and Share with Your Child

God's power is available to his people of all ages—young and old. Do you sometimes underestimate what he'll do through a child? Most adults do. Think about what he did through young David, Samuel, and Josiah. Look up Romans 12:1–2, remembering that what God is looking for is willing vessels through which to show his power and glory. Share your observations with your child.

met. Introduce yourself and your family. Tell them where you live, give them your phone number, and invite them to call anytime, even if it's just to borrow some eggs! Letting those who are close by know you care shows God's love.

Community Soup (Family activity)

Send out homemade invitations to a Community Soup block party. Include the date, time, location, and a notice that each family should contribute one large can of something to go into a tomato-base soup. Provide cornbread and have the soup base ready when guests arrive so that there will be less time to wait for dinner. Meanwhile, you can play board games, horseshoes, or softball.

Wheel Deal (Ages 7 and up)

- What's it like to be disabled? Rent or borrow a wheelchair and let your child spend the day being wheeled around at the mall or grocery store. How do store assistants treat you? Passersby? Talk about your child's discoveries.
- Assist JAF Ministries' Wheelchairs for the World campaign, which mobilizes communities and churches to collect used wheelchairs, which JAF Ministries then repairs and distributes to disabled people around the world. Contact 818-707-5664.

Giving Gifts in Secret
(All ages)

Is there a family in your neighborhood or church that's having a hard time making ends meet? Perhaps it was all they could do to pay last month's gas bill. God loves to see his children give gifts in secret (see Matt. 6). Here are some ideas on secret gift giving:

- Leave a bag of groceries on the doorstep.
- Find out a need, such as for a sweater or Sunday school clothes, and give a gift certificate anonymously at Christmas.
- Make a gift basket of "extras" that most likely would not be bought during tight times.

Journal Jots

For Your Child to Write About

- In what ways have others helped you? Perhaps a kind word was said to you or you just got an encouraging pat on the back for no special reason. How did those actions make you feel? How do those actions follow God's instruction to love each other?
- Serving God doesn't just mean full-time Christian service. We can serve God in business, schools, the arts, or many other ways. In your journal, list some ways you could serve God.

Shine on Shut-Ins
(Ages 8 and up)

Ask around your neighborhood or church to discover a family that has a bedridden loved one and spends extra time caring for them. Offer to read if the person can't see well; or offer to run an errand or mow the lawn.

On the Other Side
(All ages)

Part of living for God is not to become so attached to our material riches that we forget to seek first the kingdom. In her book, *World*

Bookworm

Resources for Children

Bratton, Heidi. *Yes, I Can!* Mahwah, N.J.:
Paulist, 1997. Walking with God
series. For ages 0–5.
Children of the Window Prayer Calendar,
Caleb Project. www.calebproject.org
(303-730-4170). For ages 3 and up.
Lorbiecki, Marybeth. *Sister Anne's Hands.*
New York: Penguin, 1998. For ages 4–
8. Shows how to respond well to
offenses while helping or loving others.
Webb, Dana. *Jared and the Ordinary,
Handy-Dandy, Excellent, Extraordinary,
Plain Brown String.* Colorado Springs:
Chariot Victor, 1999. For ages 5–10.

Proofing Your Kids, Lael Arrington talks about living the American Dream, with its ever-climaxing "lust-ometor." Learn some ways to keep your "lust-ometor" in check:

• Drive around some distressed neighborhoods (preferably during the day, with Dad), pray for the people, and ask God if there's anything he would have you do.
• Volunteer in a soup kitchen for a week or even a day.
• Offer your skills for the benefit of the poor. One woman offered tutoring services two afternoons a week to at-risk inner-city kids. She was able to give them emotional support when things went wrong at school and to be a friend to the single moms as well.

Mobilizing Kids in Missions
(All ages)

Involving children in kids-to-kids projects can be a great way to help them develop a worldview and be involved with taking the Gospel to other nations. Have your children fill shoeboxes with gifts for needy girls and boys around the world (through Samaritan's Purse's Operation Christmas Child, for instance, 800-353-5949 usa@samaritan.org). A great project for a Sunday school class, these boxes are collected and distributed all year, not just at Christmas.

Sponsor a Child
(Family activity)

As a family, sponsor a hungry child on a monthly basis through an organization like World Vision or Compassion International.

Be A Pen Pal
(Ages 8 and up)

Have your kids make cards for the children of the missionaries your church supports or offer friendship by becoming an e-mail pen pal.

Adopt a People
(Ages 6–12)

In your Sunday school class, children's church, or homeschool, focus each month on one country or unreached people group. Let kids taste the food from that area and invite an international student from that region to come for dinner and share about his or her culture and religion. Travel to that country through books and pray for the people group. Caleb Project, which focuses on unreached people groups in the 10/40 Window, has many resources for children. (Call 303-730-4170 for a catalog.)

Bookbag

Resources for Parents

Arrington, Lael F. *World Proofing Your Kids: Helping Moms Prepare Their Kids to Navigate Today's Turbulent Times.* Wheaton: Crossway, 1997.

Chapman, Gary and Ross Campbell. *Five Love Languages of Children.* Nashville: Lifeway, 1998.

Hohmann, Pete. *Mobilizing Kids for Outreach.* Springfield, Mo.: Gospel Publishing House, 1997. Video and resource notebook for taking kids on outreaches. Contact 1-800-641-4310.

Generation. Houston: Mars Hill Productions, 1996. A video about how God is using youth around the world in evangelism, prayer, and missions. www.mars-hill-media.org

Each child receives God's best gifts for the working out of His plans and purposes in that child's life, and for the benefit of other lives he will touch.

—Don and Katie Fortune,
Discovering Your Children's Gifts

What you are is God's gift to you. What you make of yourself is your gift to God.

—Anonymous

Believing in our children—and carrying out that belief through our prayers, words, and actions— unleashes them to be all they can be.
It's our privilege to cheer them forward.

—Miles McPherson,
The Power of Believing in Your Child

Fan into flame the gift of God, which is in you.

—2 Timothy 1:6

twelve

the **spiritual** gifts **window**

Christmas lights twinkled around the window in our daughter Alison's room, her handiwork to make even the bedroom festive for the holiday season. We snuggled under her comforter reading the Bible story about the rich man who had so much money, food, hay, and grain stored up that he had to build bigger barns to hold it all. The final verse of the story says the man loved all his things more than he loved God.

"God can tell if we love our stuff more than we love him," I explained. "Because if we do, we'll hang onto everything and not share the gifts he has given us."

That triggered a thought in our eight-year-old's mind as she reminded me of one of her Christmas traditions—picking out one of her favorite toys to give to a needy child. "I want to give a doll this year; my German doll or Newborn—I think that's what God wants me to give," she said.

Before I even thought, the words came out of my mouth, "Not Newborn; you've had that doll since you were a baby. And Shelly (the German doll) cost so much! How about giving your new Cabbage Patch doll or the talking doll?"

"Isn't that what we're supposed to do, Mom? The Bible says we ought to give our *best*."

> God has given each of you some special abilities; be sure to use them to help each other, passing on to others God's many kinds of blessings. Are you called to preach? Then preach as though God himself were speaking through you. Are you called to help others? Do it with all the strength and energy that God supplies, so that God will be glorified through Jesus Christ—to him be glory and power forever and ever. Amen.
>
> —1 PETER 4:10–11 lb

Ouch! I felt like God himself had asked me the question. Of course she was right, and I was convicted and humbled at my selfish thoughts. Alison did give away Shelly, her German doll, with great joy later that week, and I'm sure some little girl was thrilled as well by this gift of love.

Alison's generosity wasn't just a whim. Time after time as she was growing up, we saw her desire to give whatever she had, her thoughtfulness and creativity in choosing or making a gift, her sensitivity to the needs of others, and even her willingness to put others' needs above her own. While I was a slow learner (as the above situation shows), we found that when we encouraged Alison's giving and appreciated this tendency as a spiritual gift from God, it helped the gift bloom.

Now a young woman in her midtwenties, Alison is still giving. It may be an anonymous gift certificate to a restaurant for a couple at church that's having a difficult time, filling a need for a friend or stranger, or thoughtful gifts to me, her dad, and her siblings. Alison's not attached to her stuff but sees what she has as opportunities to bless others. Alison is a musician and has language skills, artistic talent, and counseling gifts, but her gift of giving is part of how God created her. When she's strapped financially and can't give, she's miserable. In using the gift of giving, she experiences God's presence and joy.

What Is Your Child's Spiritual Gift?

If you want your children to grow in their faith and to experience the joy of serving God, one of the best ways is to help them discover the special gifts he has given them. Spiritual gifts are tools God gives us, tools he wants to demonstrate his power through. Since his work is spiritual, the tools are spiritual also; they are what the Bible calls spiritual gifts. These gifts are not the same as natural, intellectual, or physical gifts, such as a special ability in math or the physical prowess of a gymnast. These are spiritual gifts God built into us to be used for his glory and the benefit of others. A key passage of the New Testament describes spiritual gifts: "We have different gifts, according to the grace given us. If a man's gift is prophesying, let him use it in proportion to his faith. If it is serving, let him serve; if it is teaching, let him teach; if it is encouraging, let him encourage; if it is contributing to the needs of others, let him give generously; if it is leadership, let him govern diligently; if it is showing mercy, let him do it cheerfully" (Rom. 12:6–8).

> God has given each of us the ability to do certain things well. So if God has given you the ability to prophesy, then prophesy whenever you can—as often as your faith is strong enough to receive a message from God.
>
> —ROMANS 12:6 1b

Other spiritual gifts are described in 1 Corinthians 12:7–11, Ephesians 4:11–13, and 1 Peter 4:10–11. In each of these passages, when Paul describes the gifts, he says they aren't given merely to bless the one who has the gift but to equip us for ministry and service, to show God's love and achieve his purposes, to bless and build up the body of Christ. "Each one should use whatever gift he has received to serve others, faithfully administering God's grace in its various forms," says 1 Peter 4:10. One gift isn't more important than the others. They are all needed.

Moreover, nobody is left out. When spiritual gifts were passed out by God, he gave each one of us, young and old, at least one (and usually more) way to serve. All Christians—no matter what their age—have the "grown-up" Holy Spirit. Once God's Spirit indwells a person at salvation, even if she's only six, spiritual gifts come with the package.

Most people have several gifts that could function together to serve God's purposes. For example, David was not only a faithful shepherd boy, he also composed music, sang and performed excellently, and had leadership and administrative gifts, a gift of courage, skill in warfare, and was a man after God's own heart.

Talk with your child about the following characteristics to begin to discover his spiritual gifts:[1]

- I like sharing my testimony, sharing a story about how God has worked in my life, or telling someone the Gospel. (evangelism)
- I love studying God's Word and digging in to uncover truths. (teaching)
- I spend time praying for friends, family, and others even when no one asks me to. (intercession)
- I am sensitive, perceptive, and discerning of the motives and heart purposes of other people. (prophecy)
- It's natural for me to take leadership in the classroom, in youth group, or on the playground when no one else has emerged as a leader. (administration/leadership)
- I love to help other people grow in their faith. (exhortation)
- I understand the Gospel and can easily share and explain it to others, even debating with people when there are dilemmas. (evangelism/teaching/preaching)
- I am quick to think of ways to help people and enjoy serving others. (serving)
- I like to give and enjoy giving thoughtful, unexpected, or generous gifts. (giving)

Discovering your children's spiritual gifts is a key to helping them experience the joy of serving and following Christ. It also helps them find their fit in the youth group, school, or church body that they're a part of. What fun there is when we begin discovering the ways God can best use us—not just for adults but also for children!

Miles McPherson, a former NFL football player and a powerful evangelist who ministers to thousands of youths in his Miles Ahead Crusades, describes how his spiritual gifts emerged: "When I was young, I loved to argue—especially with my family—about anything and everything. Even if I had no idea what I was talking about, I invented a reason to argue. I can see now that God was preparing a preacher who would be ready to argue for the sake of the Gospel. He was training me to present the Good News with passion, conviction, and urgency, not wanting anyone to be lost. I'm still competitive and hate to lose a debate. To me, every sermon is an argument with someone who believes the devil's point of view."[2]

Discovering the Gifts

Miles didn't just suddenly have the gift for preaching when he turned twenty-five and began his crusades. It was there from the time he was very young. "Even in young children, the various gifts begin to focus on meeting specific human needs," write Don and Katie Fortune.[3] And as children mature, so do their gifts and their capacity to use them to meet needs.

If we're observant and sensitive to our kids in the everyday encounters of our family, we'll begin to see their spiritual gifts in action. As the Johnson family was seated around the table for a birthday dinner one evening, Jana, the youngest sister, spilled her milk and the glass went shattering across the wood floor. Patty, the middle child, ran over and grabbed a towel from the kitchen. "Oh, it won't take long to clean up. I'll fix it; don't worry, Jana," Patty said as she mopped up milk from the floor. As usual, Patty wanted to be a helper. She's sensitive to other people's needs and wants to accomplish jobs quickly—evidence of a spiritual gift of serving.

Now God gives us many kinds of special abilities, but it is the same Holy Spirit who is the source of them all. … To one person the Spirit gives the ability to give wise advice; someone else may be especially good at studying and teaching, and this is his gift from the same Spirit. He gives special faith to another, and to someone else the power to heal the sick.

—1 CORINTHIANS 12: 4,8–9 lb

Before Mom and Dad could get the words out of their mouths, Wendy said, "Don't do that; you might cut yourself on the broken glass! Get the broom first. And Jana, if you'd keep your glass away from the edge of the table like I told you yesterday, it wouldn't have happened."

As Jana started to cry, Rachel, the next-door neighbor's child who was over for dinner, put her arm around Jana and comforted her, "Don't cry; I've spilled my milk lots of times."

> Every desirable and beneficial gift comes out of heaven. The gifts are rivers of light cascading down from the Father of Light.
>
> —JAMES 1:17 message

Just as Patty was acting out of her gift of serving, well-meaning Wendy was exhibiting her gifts of administration (telling Patty what to do) and teaching ("keep your glass away from the edge"). And by gently comforting her milk-spilling friend, Rachel was operating out of the gift of mercy.

As we can see in this family scenario, just as the gifts have positive sides, they also have negative ones. Like Miles, someone who's argumentative might have the talent to be a preacher, an evangelist, or an apologist like Ravi Zacharius or Chuck Colson, who defends the Christian faith in an unbelieving world.

A person with an administrative gift, like Wendy, can appear bossy or get upset when others don't work toward the goal she's set; and someone with a serving gift can try to take over and manage things. A child gifted with compassion is sensitive, gets his feelings hurt easily, and can get overwhelmed with the suffering of others.[4] A person with a teaching bent can instruct in a "know it all" way instead of encouraging someone, like Jana, who already feels badly about what she's done. And sometimes we compare ourselves to others with "better" gifts and find ourselves feeling either inferior or superior.

Maybe that's why Paul says in his discussion of spiritual gifts in Romans 12:6, "Let's just go ahead and be what we were made to be, without enviously or pridefully comparing ourselves with each other, or trying to be something we aren't" (MESSAGE).

The more we can help our children understand their spiritual gifts, the more they can grow and serve, not comparing themselves to others but using their God-given gifts. As we hold out a bright future for them, they will have hope that they can make a difference. And as they learn to rely on God and use their spiritual gifts, ordinary kids can accomplish the extraordinary.

Making a World of Difference

A twelve-year-old Canadian boy named Craig Kielburger read in the newspaper one morning about a boy just his age in Pakistan who was murdered for speaking out against child labor. The article described how the boy, Iqbal, was taken out of school, sold into labor at age four as a carpet weaver to pay his father's debt, and then was murdered when he spoke out about the conditions he and many children like him had suffered under.

That day Craig's heart went out to Iqbal and the others like him described in the article. Craig couldn't get out of his mind the images of kids forced to work in mines, factories, and the sex trade. He was so moved with compassion that he did more research and discovered that Iqbal was one of over 250 million child laborers around the world who get no education, have no freedom, and live in poverty and abuse.

> It is God himself who has made us what we are and given us new lives from Christ Jesus; and long ages ago he planned that we should spend these lives in helping others.
>
> —EPHESIANS 2:10 lb

Craig decided to do something to stop the cruelty. His parents listened, encouraged him, and brainstormed with him about what could be done. The idea of a kids' organization to fight child labor emerged, which he then took to school. And after sharing with his seventh-grade class the plight of child laborers, Craig and his friends started Free the Children. Although many adults said the children couldn't make a difference, Craig prayed and took it step by step.

By raising funds with garage sales and car washes, by acting through petitions and letter-writing campaigns, and eventually through writing a book, speaking, and maintaining a website, Craig and Free the Children have contributed to new legislation designed to protect children in several countries and have raised awareness around the world of the problem of child labor. And through his gift of mercy (and administration, as he managed the organization Free the Children, and exhortation, as he spoke out against child labor and challenged adults and kids to get involved in doing something), this twelve-year-old accomplished amazing things.[5]

> Christ has given each of us special abilities—whatever he wants us to have out of his rich storehouse of gifts. The Psalmist tells about this, for he says that when Christ returned triumphantly to heaven after his resurrection and victory over Satan, he gave generous gifts to men....
>
> —EPHESIANS 4:7–8, 11 lb

Can a child's evangelistic gift make a difference? Monica, a ten-year-old in Bogotá, Colombia, along with the other children in grades two through six at her church, was taught to share her faith in Jesus Christ in a kids' version of Evangelism Explosion. But Monica didn't just listen like the rest of the kids. Because of her heart for lost people, she quietly began singing the songs she had learned and practicing Bible verses on the two-hour hot, dusty bus ride to and from school each day.

In a few weeks, one of the passengers on the bus asked her where the songs came from. She told him they came from the Bible and recited the words along with other truths she had learned in the program. She just offered the little she had. As the passengers became more open to hearing Monica's songs and Bible verses, she developed more confidence in talking to them about Jesus. And she eventually shared the Gospel with every adult she regularly rode with. In doing so, Monica realized that she enjoyed sharing her faith in Christ more than talking about almost anything.

Finally, after hearing Monica for several weeks, a man on the bus said he believed and prayed to trust Christ alone—not good works or just going to church and participating in the rituals or reciting a liturgy—for his salvation. A few days later, another person committed her life to Christ. Before long, the bus driver stopped the bus by the side of the road, listened as Monica shared the truth, and then he and all ten of the passengers left on the bus prayed a prayer of commitment. Even though Monica lived in one of the poorest barrios in Bogotá, she invited the converts to her home to learn more about Jesus. Her parents led a Bible study with the new believers, and within a few months, the group grew into a church called Iglesia Cruzada Cristiana, which now has approximately 500 members and is still growing—all because of the spiritual gifts and boldness of a little girl.

> Some of us have been given special ability as apostles; to others he has given the gift of being able to preach well; some have special ability in winning people to Christ, helping them to trust him as their Savior; still others have a gift for caring for God's people as a shepherd does his sheep, leading and teaching them in the ways of God.
>
> —Ephesians 4:11 1b

Don't Bury the Gift

When we give our little, as Monica did or as the little boy in John 6:9 did when he offered the fish and loaves of bread, we can serve many and can accomplish much. But lots of kids (and adults) operate like the servant who buried his talent did in the parable of the talents (Matt. 25:14–30). Through fear of failure or unwillingness to risk or invest their efforts, they don't use the gifts and talents God gave them. But sometimes they don't use their gifts simply because they aren't aware of the value and treasure God has deposited in them.

Parents can make a world of difference in how kids see themselves by recognizing and encouraging their spiritual gifts. One day our daughter's friend Julie was at our house for a sleepover. I was preparing dinner when Julie came in and asked how she could help. After I got over the shock (I didn't get these offers of help all the time), I said, "You could cut up those carrots and celery and make the salad if you want to."

Julie happily worked beside me. When she finished the salad, she asked if she could set the table.

"Thanks for your help, Julie!" I said.

"Oh, that's okay. I enjoyed it. Mom's pointed out that God has given me a gift of serving, and I've realized I'm happiest when I'm helping someone!"

This child was developing a healthy sense of worth and value as she began to see how God had designed her and created her for a purpose. At a young age, she began to use her spiritual gifts and experienced much joy in the process.

Helping your children unwrap their spiritual gifts isn't an unreachable task. Discovering ways to serve God and help others can give your children a taste for the goodness of God and the joy of being used by him and can enable them to bless the lives of others. Fanning into flame the gifts of God within your kids, as 2 Timothy 1:6 suggests, can yield much fruit, both in their lives and in the lives of those they serve and reach out to.

Making the Most of the Spiritual Gifts Window

Unwrapping the Gifts
(Ages 8 and up)

Look up the four major passages in the Bible that discuss spiritual gifts.: Romans 12:6–8; 1 Corinthians 12:7–10; 2 Corinthians 9:12–14; and Ephesians 4:11. Write the verses on index cards. Put each passage in a package and wrap it up (or put it in a gift bag). Then have your children unwrap the packages and discover the spiritual gifts listed in the passage: serving, teaching, encouragement, evangelism, preaching, giving, and so on, and talk about what the words mean. Then pray for your children, asking God to reveal how he has gifted each one, praying for the release of the gifts and for his blessing on their lives. Pray that as they discover and use their gifts, God will get the glory and they will experience his joy.

Movie Night
(All ages)

Rent a video of the movie *Chariots of Fire* and zero in on the scene in which Eric Liddell is talking with his sister Jennie on the hill and explains to her that God has made him fast and that when he runs, he feels God's pleasure. Then ask, "What are some things you can think of that when you do them, you feel God's pleasure?" This can be a key to your child's gifts.

Jump In!
(Ages 7 and up)

Trying out different tasks, ministries, and projects gives young people a chance to find out what they enjoy and what they don't enjoy, what's easeful and full of grace and what is sheer drudgery. Give your child opportunities to choose some of the things he participates in and what he's going to do in a family project. Encourage him to try something different if he always does the same thing and to exercise his spiritual gifts as they are recognized. It might be writing a puppet script for an inner-city vacation Bible school, praying for missionaries, or organizing

Heart to Heart

Think It Over and Share with Your Child

- What are your spiritual gifts? Share with your child a time when you used your gifts and someone was blessed.
- Do you pray for health and success for your child or for God to use him in his great purposes for the life of the world?
- Most parents don't see their children as God sees them, with the spiritual capabilities and potential that they have. Ask God to help you, through Christ-colored glasses, to glimpse the purposes he has for each of them.

a party. Another time it might be volunteering to teach one segment of Bible study at his school.

Treasure Hunt
(All ages)

Get a fresh perspective of your kids. As parents, we know them so well—warts and all—that sometimes we miss the treasures and gifts that may be dormant within them. Apply Philippians 4:8–9 to your vision of your child, "[Meditate] on things true, noble, reputable, authentic, compelling, gracious—the best, not the worst; the beautiful, not the ugly; things to praise, not things to curse.... Do that, and God, who makes everything work together, will work you into his most excellent harmonies" (MESSAGE). It may be in a young, unpolished, unfinished vessel, but God has deposited gifts in your kids. Ask him to show you. Then list what good things you see—a gentle spirit, compassion, leadership, a desire to help people know God, musical talent, serving or teaching gifts. In your gift list include natural talents like music, computers, art, sports, and so on.

Journal Jots

For Your Child to Write About

Laura Ingalls Wilder said, "We must first see the vision in order to realize it; we must have the ideal or we cannot approach it. But when once the dream is dreamed, it is time to wake up and get busy. We must do great deeds, not dream them all day long." Write down some of your dreams and hopes for the future.

Dream Maker
(All ages)

A child's dreams can be evidence of God's call and gifting in their life. Joseph's dream of rulership, though it incensed his brothers and led to his being sold as a slave in Egypt, was indicative of his gifting and purpose in life. Talk with your children or teens about their dreams and hopes for the future. No matter how big the dream may seem, don't throw cold water on it by ridiculing or criticizing. Instead, pray for their dreams, pray that they will delight in the Lord and that he will give them the desire of their heart (Ps. 37:4). Ask God to reveal to your children his destiny and vision for their lives. Encourage them that as they trust and follow God and the light he gives, dreams can come true.

Skill Building
(All ages)

Even if someone is gifted by God, they still need to develop skills so as to do their work or ministry "heartily, as to the Lord" (Col. 3:23 NKJV) and excellently so that God will be glorified. If your child shows signs of a particular gift, look for classes, opportunities, books, or resources that could help her develop skills. Encourage her when she stretches to meet a challenge and makes mistakes or fails. And if her gift is in an area in which you are deficient or uninterested, find a mentor at your church or in the community who could teach your child. Water the gifts with encouraging words, prayers, actions, opportunities, and time. Remember to be patient, because it takes time for young people to grow into their gifts.

Widen Your View of the Spiritual Capacity of Kids (For parents)

We often limit children by our small perspective of their potential and spiritual capacity. Look up the following passages that describe how

Bookworm

Resources for Children

Haidle, Helen. *What Would Jesus Do?* Grand Rapids: Zondervan, 1997. Charles Sheldon's classic, *In His Steps,* retold for children. For ages 5–12.

_____. *What Would Jesus Do Today?* Grand Rapids: Zondervan, 2000. A one-year devotional. For ages 5–12.

Osborne, Rick, and K. Christie Bowler. *Who Is Sam Harrington?* Grand Rapids: Zondervan, 2000. For ages 4–8.

Today's Heroes book series. Grand Rapids: Zondervan. Individual paperback books on true heroes of today. For ages 8–12.

God used some children and young people in his plan in a mighty
way:

> David, who was a boy when he struck down Goliath (1 Sam-
> uel 17)
> Josiah, who became King of Judah at age eight and turned his
> nation back to God by the time he was twenty-six, against
> many odds (2 Kings 22:1–23:30)
> Esther, who saved God's people from extinction (the book of
> Esther)
> Jeremiah, who was young when God called him (Jeremiah 1)

Support from Heaven
(Ages 3 and up)

With your child, look at two verses. The first, in 2 Chronicles
16:9, says, "The eyes of the LORD range throughout the earth to
strengthen [to show Himself strong, to fully support] those whose
hearts are fully committed to him." Next look up Romans 12:1. God
is looking for willing vessels who are surrendered to him. Ask your
child, "Will you be that heart that is fully committed to his purposes?" If so, hold on tight, because the adventure of a lifetime will
begin.

Act It Out
(Ages 3–14)

From a contemporary or easy-to-read translation, read with your
children the parable of the talents in Matthew 25:14–30. Then assign
parts and, using makeshift costumes, act out the story. Afterward,
discuss what kinds of things can hinder us from using our talents.

Curl Up and Read
(Ages 3–14)

Get some of the books in the Today's Heroes book series pub-
lished by Zondervan (listed in Bookworm: Resources for Children).
As you read aloud together of extraordinary people like Dave
Dravecky, Ben Carson, Joni E. Tada, and Heather Whitestone, look

not only at the person's talent in dance, baseball, or medicine but also at the spiritual gifts they had and how God used them in his greater plan for their life.

Pray Big!
(All ages)

In Brazil, a movement called Wake Up, Deborah! has mobilized mothers to pray their children and teenagers out of harm's way and onto the mission field. They don't just ask God to give their kids a comfortable lifestyle of church-going, but they ask that he would use their lives for his purpose in fulfilling the Great Commission. Don't just pray for health, good grades, success, or a winning track season

Resources for Parents

Fortune, Don and Katie. *Discovering Your Children's Spiritual Gifts.* Grand Rapids: Chosen, 1989. Includes excellent surveys to help determine the spiritual gifts of your children, preschoolers through teenagers.

Gangel, Kenneth O. *Unwrap Your Spiritual Gifts.* Colorado Springs: Chariot/Victor, 1983.

Swindoll, Chuck. *He Gave Gifts.* Frisco, Tex.: Insight for Living, 1999. Cassette series and study guide. www.insight.org or 800-772-8888.

for your child. With the list you made for the Treasure Hunt activity, pray for God to use the gifts and strengths of your child for his glory. Pray for him to put your child in the place in the Kingdom that he's designed them for, to function with maximum joy and effectiveness, and for all that he's planned in heaven for them to be done on earth as they grow, live, and serve.

God intends and desires for your children to grow up in Him that they will desire to have faith children of their own, continuing the progeny of God from one generation to many generations, until the people of God are too numerous to count.

—Phil Phillips,
Helping Your Children Walk with God

I will reveal these truths to you so that you can describe these glorious deeds of Jehovah to your children, and tell them about the mighty miracles he did. For he gave his laws to Israel, and commanded our fathers to teach them to their children, so that they in turn could teach their children too. Thus his laws pass down from generation to generation. In this way each generation has been able to obey his laws and to set its hope anew on God and not forget his glorious miracles.

—Psalm 78:4–7 LB

God has had your mission of raising godly kids in his mind from the beginning of time, and he wants you to succeed even more than you do.

—Bruce Wilkinson,
Experiencing Spiritual Breakthroughs:
The Powerful Principle of the Three Chairs

thirteen

the **heritage** window

This week I saw and heard the most amazing thing—five of the best young musicians I've ever heard in concert, all from the same family: The Wolavers, who live in Nashville, Tennessee.

A number of years ago, when they had only three children, I interviewed Robin, the mom, and wrote a story, called "The Baby Who Loved Opera," about the musical development of her first child. When she was pregnant with Annie, Robin was practicing operatic arias every day for her master's degree in vocal music. Opera, you could say, was Annie's musical environment in utero; she heard it by natural surround sound in her mother's womb.

So when Annie first began singing "Jesus Loves Me" and "Old MacDonald" as a toddler, she sang the songs in perfect pitch with a distinctly operatic style (which caused her Sunday school teachers quite a few chuckles!). At the age of ten, after a few years of violin lessons, Annie was playing the violin like an angel and won a spot as a roving violinist at a Laura Ashley store at Christmas and other awards as well. At thirteen, she won the Blount Concerto Competition and performed the Mendelssohn violin concerto with the Montgomery Symphony. She was chosen as first violinist of the Brahms Quintet—which debuted at New York's Lincoln Center—and, at sixteen, attends the Juilliard precollege program in New York City. One of the most promising young violinists in the country, Annie's performance at the concert I attended was stunning.

But that wasn't the most amazing thing. It wasn't just one super-talented child I heard—but a whole family of musicians. Alex, fourteen, and Benjamin, twelve, played cello, Camille, nine, played piano and violin, and Gretchen, six, played a miniature violin. Three-year-old Jeremiah, although he shows great talent, has yet to pick his instrument. He happily sang along with the group.

> You have heard my vows, O God; you have given me the heritage of those who fear your name.
>
> —Psalm 61:5

As the Wolavers performed, I witnessed something more than the performance of a nice wonderful repertoire of music by some young talented players.

I saw *heritage*.

These weren't nominal musicians. They really seemed to thoroughly enjoy performing and did it with excellence. Their parents had passed along a heritage, a rich legacy of music, to their six children.

How did they do it?

A Family That Played Together

When their children were very young, the Wolavers introduced them to instruments and let them choose one for their very own. Robin and her husband, both musicians and songwriters, were intentional about passing on their musical heritage and committed to pursuing music as a family—and not just on Sundays. They didn't want their kids to be just spectators—hearing their parents' compositions or merely listening to CDs of other musicians' performances. They wanted their children to follow in their footsteps as music-makers, but they also hoped their kids would surpass their achievements.

So the Wolavers took their kids to lessons, provided the instruments and ample practice time, spent hours listening to them and encouraging them in their mistakes and triumphs, and played with them for fun at home so that making music was a family pastime. It took a tremendous investment of time; they had to sacrifice other activities, and there were many stops and starts and disappointments.

But what a fruitful harvest! The children aren't all grown up yet; but we can get a glimpse of where they're headed and how they are beginning to surpass their parents' accomplishments. Along with Annie, Alex and Benjamin also attend the Juilliard pre-college program. Alex and Annie were joint winners last year in their concerto competition. Who knows what they'll do in the music world? They've taken the baton (or the violin, to be more accurate) and aren't just moving around the track—they're already hitting their stride.

It remains to be seen what the musical accomplishments and destiny will be for each of the Wolaver children. But they've got a great foundation and are well on their way, not only with music but also, I should mention, in the Christian life.

> These commandments that I give you today are to be upon your hearts. Impress them on your children. Talk about them when you sit at home and when you walk along the road, when you lie down and when you get up.
>
> —DEUTERONOMY 6:6–7

Passing On a Spiritual Heritage

Passing on our spiritual heritage is not unlike passing on the value of music, as the Wolavers are doing with their children. To pass on our spiritual heritage, we must build a spiritual environment at home, model a good example, be intentional about relating to God and teaching biblical foundations, and enjoy God as individuals and as a family.

But as important as music is for the Wolavers, it's not the bottom line. "Music is a great gift to us and we hope to glorify God with our instruments and voices. But our greatest desire is that our children know and love God above all. If our ability to make music is taken away, God is still our rock bottom," said Robin to the audience between numbers. "If we lose loved ones or material things, God is still our strong foundation. He's the reason for everything we do."

What does it mean to pass on a Christian heritage? Third John 4 says it well, "I have no greater joy than to hear that my children are walking in the truth." It means raising children who grow up with God—who not only enjoy the Lord and love him but also have chosen to walk in his truth—following and serving him with their own lives—just as we've been talking about throughout the pages of this book.

> Since my youth, O God, you have taught me, and to this day I declare your marvelous deeds. Even when I am old and gray, do not forsake me, O God, till I declare your power to the next generation, your might to all who are to come.
>
> —Psalm 71:17–18

"Ultimately, the goal of the Father for your children is not only that they come to know Christ as their Savior, not only that they know and believe his mighty works, not only that they know and obey his inspired Word, but that they choose of their own free will to love and serve him," says Bruce Wilkinson in his book *Experiencing Spiritual Breakthroughs*.[1]

There couldn't be any more important responsibility for parents! Yet many people in our society urge us not to force our beliefs on our kids but instead to invest all our parenting time in education, sports, computers, and video entertainment. Let children decide for themselves, find their own truths, study other religions, and pick the one that fits their needs.

"To many parents, freedom of religion means freedom *from religion*," says John Drescher. "They spend their time accumulating wealth instead of building character. Some have accepted the fallacy that they should not teach religion to the child, lest the child be prejudiced. Let the child choose, they say." But the absence of teaching about God leaves a spiritual vacuum in a child's heart and he becomes "a prey of all kinds of false gods and philosophies."[2]

The Power of Spiritual Heritage

In contrast, when spiritual heritage is passed on from parents to children, it's a lifesaving, life-giving force, a source of hope, purpose, and meaning that transcends the painful and tragic events of life. Just ask Everett Alvarez Jr., a navy pilot who was shot down over North

Vietnam in 1964. Alvarez spent eight and a half years as a prisoner of war in brutal and inhumane conditions.

Alvarez didn't have a chapel to retreat to when he felt broken or discouraged from interrogation or torture; he didn't have a pastor to comfort or encourage him when he was lonely and the nights seemed endless. So the first Sunday after being imprisoned, he created his own worship space.

With an old rusty nail, he carved a foot-high cross on a courtyard wall near his cell, and under it, he scratched his name and the date he was shot down. Every day thereafter, Alvarez held worship services before the cross, which he could see through bars above the door of his prison cell.

> Train a child in the way he should go, and when he is old he will not turn from it.
>
> —PROVERBS 22:6

Where did the second-longest-held captive of the Vietnam War get the spiritual strength to survive month after month, year after year, with his faith and hope intact? From the spiritual heritage passed on by his parents and church.

Because he had gone to church with his family and had been an altar boy, Alvarez could recall many Scriptures and prayers. Along with these verses, he recited the Lord's Prayer and the Apostles' Creed daily during his time with God. The navy pilot had received a legacy of prayer and faith from his parents, and "prayer helped sustain me through those long days and nights, and through the brutal interrogations in the room next door," he said. He didn't rail against God, give up, or deny him. He held fast to the spiritual heritage that had been passed down to him and to the God he'd known from his childhood.[3]

The Ultimate Mission

If you're an NBA coach and take your focus off winning the championship, stop caring about the next game, stop practicing, and think that your players can coast, you're headed for a loss. Your mission is the NBA championship; your eyes have to stay on the prize to succeed.

The same goes for many other high-level sports and professional careers. For a medical degree, you have premed courses in college and a difficult entrance exam, the MCAT. Then you face four intensive years of study in medical school and grueling years of training during internship and residency. You have to keep your eyes on the prize and focus on the big picture and the high calling. If you don't keep the goal in mind, you'll give up.

> We no longer believe just because of what you said; now we have heard for ourselves, and we know that this man really is the Savior of the world.
>
> —JOHN 4:42

The same is true for passing on a spiritual heritage to our children. It's a long journey. It takes years of investment. Yet it's even more important than an NBA championship or any professional degree. In fact, it's the ultimate mission.

If we don't slack off, if we do something each day to open our children's spiritual windows, to share truth while we're in transit, and to help our kids connect regularly with God as they grow, they can increase in the grace and knowledge of Christ. Sure, there will be blips and interruptions, and your child may not fully commit until he's twenty or thirty, but if we train him in the way he should go, the foundation will be laid.

The big picture is even larger than we might imagine. The point is that we open our children's spiritual windows not so they'll be happier, more comfortable, or more successful in the world but so they'll walk in devotion, know Jesus intimately, receive his everlasting love, and enter into partnership with him in his Great Commission so that they'll walk in the incredible destiny he has for them. That's a goal worth living for.

Yet we can't force our children to fall in love with God. We can't make them be godly people. It happens, instead, through the gentle moving of the Holy Spirit within them. It happens as God's Word comes alive to them, line by line and precept by precept. It happens as we pray and surrender ourselves to God over and over, so that

he can shape us into the parents he knows our kids need. It also happens in spite of our failures.

"Our desire is to have a godly child. But that is something over which we ultimately have no control. Our *goal* is to be godly parents. That is an outcome over which we *do* have control and need to make daily choices to pursue," says Lael Arrington in *World Proofing Your Kids.*[4]

Make a plan. Maybe to read the *One-Year Bible* aloud with your child this year, to go on a mission trip or serve at a soup kitchen as a family, to memorize a chapter of the New Testament together, verse by verse, but be intentional about spiritual parenting. Choose a family devotional that helps your kids grow in their faith and add some fun to teaching times. Do something each day. Look for chances to apply God's Word to your kids' everyday experiences. You may not finish everything you attempt. You may blow it occasionally, by setting a poor example or missing family devotions, for instance, but ask God to redeem your mistakes and help you get back on the path toward the prize of the high calling—passing on your spiritual heritage to your kids.

> As for me and my household, we will serve the LORD.
>
> —JOSHUA 24:15

It's All about Discipleship

Steve was reading to his boys, ages six and four, from the book of John where Jesus said, "I am the vine; you are the branches.... Apart from me you can do nothing" (John 15:5).

"Boys, what does Jesus mean by that?" Steve asked. All he got were shoulder shrugs. "I dunno, Dad."

"Follow me and I'll show you," he said, leading his little guys to the front yard flowerbed where the English ivy grew. He first showed them a long, healthy vine (our heart, he explained), it's connection to the main branch (Jesus), and its connection to the roots underground (God in heaven, whom we have not yet seen). He explained

the importance of water (the power of the Holy Spirit). Then Steve cut off the vine and left it on the walkway.

Each day they examined the vine together and observed changes. The first few days nothing looked very different, but soon the branch was dry and withered. Isaac and Noah got it. They knew what Jesus meant when he said, "Apart from me your life is useless."

Steve and his wife, Joy, want their children to know and love God, to have a relationship with our heavenly Father, *not* a religion. So they go about the work of discipleship daily, explaining to their kids that relationship is a free gift from God to treasure and nurture, while religion is a design of man you must "work" for within an "appropriate" procedure. There's freedom with the first; bondage with the latter. They let their kids see them give thanks for the small things, struggle with attitudes, and ask for help.

The boys might burst into their parents' bedroom to show off a Lego creation and find them praying together. Joy tells the children, "You are God's great idea!" and shares how the Lord wrote all about them in his book even before he put them in their family. How he got a great idea one day to make a lovely little girl, Elizabeth, how he decided to paint her eyes brown and give her a beautiful smile and a personality that would tickle the hearts of everyone she meets. The kids listen in wide-eyed wonder, waiting to hear "their story." They want to know this God who loves them so and whom Daddy and Mommy get so excited about.

Steve and Joy also endeavor to help their children know God's Word and read it as essential nutrition for the soul. Word by word, chapter by chapter, they read and discuss, praying all the while that as their children grow, they will choose the God their parents have chosen for them.

This is how we pass on a spiritual heritage, as we lead our kids from enjoying God to loving him, following him, and serving him. As Art Murphy, author of *The Faith of a Child,* says, "It takes about fifteen minutes to bring a child to Christ; it takes five years to help him become a disciple."

Families Sharing Their Faith Together

Let me share a secret for those of you whose children are in middle school or older; maybe like Joy and Steve, you've already built a solid foundation. Now what? If you want to pass on a dynamic spiritual heritage so that your kids own their faith and don't try to ride into heaven on your spiritual coattails, let them give their faith away! Share Christ as a family. Don't just talk about faith. Don't just leave them to lounge in the valley of verse-learning and years of Sunday school. Don't tell them to wait until they're grown-up for God to use them. Discover what it's like to share God's love *together,* so they can have some peak experiences. As the Nike commercial says, "Just do it!"

> I know whom I have believed, and am convinced that he is able to guard what I have entrusted to him for that day.
>
> —2 TIMOTHY 1:12

Larry Schweitzer, a children's pastor in Naperville, Illinois, specializes in showing parents and kids how to share God's love with others. Last summer, when he took a group of thirty-four people, ranging in age from four years old to college age, he saw the effects of equipping parents and kids to give their faith away (or share their faith).

After a year of training, in which parents and kids learned ballooning, face painting, and how to prepare and share their testimony, practiced Spanish praise songs, and created a drama, the intergenerational mission group headed for Mexico. The results were amazing. Not only did many people in Juárez receive Christ as a result of the children and adults giving their faith away but the participating families were impacted as well. Children came back so fired up that they shared the Gospel with their friends and couldn't wait for the next family mission trip. Kids and parents grew closer in their relationships. Larry's own children—Brent and Alicia, twelve and thirteen—began initiating spiritual conversations with classmates at school. And one family who went on the mission trip now feels called to help plant a Hispanic church in their city.

What they found is that as parents model sharing Christ and as children have a chance to participate and see God work, the parents pass the baton of faith to their children in ways that just another youth program or vacation Bible school doesn't.

Making the Most of the Heritage Window

Throughout this book, I've provided many creative ways to open your child's spiritual windows and thus pass on your spiritual heritage. The ideas in this chapter are heritage-builders to put the icing on the cake.

Walk in Forgiveness
(All ages)

"Whether we will be heard or not depends perhaps most on the context of our advice, namely a good relationship and a good example," says Lael Arrington.[5] The number one factor that most often drives children (raised in Christian homes) away from pursuing a relationship with Christ is "injured relationships" between parents and kids.[6]

If you've inadvertently wounded your children or you have a broken relationship with one of them, seek God's healing. Ask their forgiveness for what you did (or didn't do) in the past and walk in forgiveness and openness in the future. With a healed relationship, you can begin to build bridges across which spiritual values can pass. In addition, the example you'll be giving—as one who asks forgiveness of

Heart to Heart

Think It Over and Share with Your Child

What is your great hope for your kids spiritually? Where do you want them to be in their walk with God in five years, ten years, twenty years? Perhaps share your hopes with your children. Then think about what you will need to add to your training regimen so that you will go the distance and successfully pass on the baton of faith to them.

others—will be worth more than one hundred sermons on the subject.

Share Your Personal History and Experience with God
(For parents)

Write out your own testimony or faith story of how you came to know Christ and grow in him. You can include your childhood background, the stepping stones to faith or situations that God used to draw

---

Journal Jots

For Your Child to Write About

Write in your journal an event or situation in your life or family that shows God's faithfulness. Recalling God's past faithfulness will strengthen you for trials and disappointments you may face in the future.

---

you to him, what your life before knowing Christ was like, and what your life was like after committing your life to him. Share this with your children and then have a prayer of thanksgiving for God's goodness in your life. Often kids don't know what parents were like "B.C.," or Before Christ. Fill them in on the most important family history of all!

Share Your Faith As a Family
(All ages)

Let your children see and hear you share your testimony with someone outside the family—it could be at an outreach event your church puts on, a Bible study, or a mission trip (across town or to a different city or country). Encourage them to write their own testimonies, no matter how brief they may be, so they'll be prepared to share it with others. Brainstorm on how you could share Christ with someone who's never heard the Gospel.

What's Your Heritage?
(For parents)

Find out the stories of your parents, grandparents, and great-grandparents and tell them to your children. Were they people who served and loved God? If not, are you and your children turning a "spiritual corner" so you can pass on a godly heritage?

Pass It On
(Ages 5 and up)

Bookworm

Resources for Children

ten Boom, Corrie. *The Hiding Place.* New York: Bantam, 1984. Also available as a video you can rent which tells the story of Corrie ten Boom's Dutch family, who were sent to a Nazi prison camp for hiding Jews during World War II. In this story, you see the incredible Christian heritage that was passed down to Corrie, the survivor who took the Gospel around the world to millions of people. For ages 10 and up.

Lewis, C. S. *The Chronicles of Narnia.* One of our children's all-time favorite book and audiotape series; it gave us great opportunities to discuss timeless truths while driving down the road on trips. For ages 6 and up.

McLachlan, Patricia. *All the Places to Love.* New York: HarperCollins, 1994. Depicts family harmony. For ages 5 to 8.

Wade, Mary Dobson. *Homesteading on the Plains: Daily Life in the Land of L. I. Wilder.* Brookfield, Conn.: Milbrook, 1997. For elementary age children.

Take a trip to the local Christian bookstore and look at the different faith-sharing tools available: wordless book colors by Child Evangelism, Evangicube (like the Rubic's cube but a great visual tool to share Christ even with someone of another language), power bracelets, and many others. Pick one tool and then practice with your child until she can use it to share the Good News.

Time Capsule
(Family activity)

Every five to ten years, make a family time capsule. Decorate a shoebox. Put in favorite photos, heights of children, important family Scriptures, recordings of kids and parents singing favorite songs or hymns, baby hair, handprints, and other treasures. Store the time capsule somewhere where it will be preserved.

Passing On the Gospel
without Leaving Home
(Family activity)

Invite international students or families over for a

Christmas, Thanksgiving, or Easter meal with your family. Whether your guests are from Hindu, Buddhist, or Muslim religious backgrounds, explain what the holiday means and how and why you cel-

Resources for Parents

Bruner, Kurt, and Jim Weidmann. *Family Night Tool Chest: Basic Christian Beliefs*. Colorado Springs: Focus on the Family, 1999. Look for other Heritage Builder resources from Focus on the Family.

Fuller, Cheri. *When Families Pray: 40 Devotions to Build, Strengthen, and Bond*. Sisters, Ore.: Multnomah, 1999. Forty bite-size devotions that will connect you, your child, and God heart to heart and aid you in passing on Christian faith.

Family Walk. Atlanta: Walk Thru the Bible. A monthly topical family devotional guide. Call 800-868-9300 or go to www.walkthru.org.

Ferguson, David and Teresa, et al. *Intimate Family Moments: Lessons from Galilee, Drawing Your Family Closer to God and One Another*. Wheaton: Victor, 1995. Many fun, creative ideas for family times from preschool to high school that build intimacy and a personal relationship with God.

Gaither, Gloria, and Shirley Dobson. *Let's Make a Memory*. Colorado Springs: Focus on the Family/Tyndale House, 1994.

Schweizer, Lawrence, and Julie Andersen. *Beginning Your Faith Journey*. Naperville, Ill.: self-published, 2001. To order, e-mail lchildren@aol.com.

_____. *Growing in Your Faith Journey*. Naperville, Ill.: self-published, 1999. To order, e-mail lchildren@aol.com.

_____. *Sharing Your Faith Journey*. Naperville, Ill.: self-published, 2001. To order, e-mail lchildren@aol.com.

Wilkinson, Bruce. *Experiencing Spiritual Breakthroughs: The Powerful Principle of the Three Chairs*. Sisters, Ore.: Multnomah, 1999.

ebrate it as Christians. As you share the timeless truths behind your traditions and values, not only will your guests be hearing the Gospel, but your children will as well.

Who Told You?
(Family activity)

Through the centuries, God has trusted his story to people—who will tell other people. Part of your heritage are your spiritual fathers and mothers. They may be people different than your biological mom and dad. Even if you come from a family of pagans or agnostics, you have all kinds of spiritual heritage behind you—people who passed on the Gospel from one to another until it got to you. It could be a Sunday school teacher or Young Life leader. Share these stories with your children. Consider declaring a "Spiritual Mothers/Fathers Day" where you write thank-you cards to the people who told each member of your family about Jesus.

a last **word** of encouragement

Think of the joy you would feel if your child hit a grand slam, bringing the three runners on base all the way home and winning the game. You'd throw your hat in the air, cheer and scream with the fans, and feel a rush you wouldn't believe! Think of the sheer delight you'd experience if your son or daughter walked across the stage and received the highest academic or military honors. Think of the thrill you'd feel if your child won an Olympic gold medal. As parents, we'd be beside ourselves with joy.

But there is a greater joy. With all my heart I believe—and have experienced—that 3 John 4 is true: "I have no greater joy than to hear that my children are walking in the truth."

No greater joy in the whole world.

To see your son loving his wife and God passionately; to watch them pray with and for their little children and teach them God's ways. To see your daughter and son-in-law following and serving God by discipling junior-high kids or sharing Christ in the place they work. To hear of the compassion your grown children extend in their workplace or neighborhood that touches people's hearts and lets them know that God loves them.

That's the big picture, and it's not an impossible dream. As I've shared throughout this book, our most important job—that of growing in our Christian faith and sharing our faith with our children so they will learn to enjoy, love, follow, and serve God—is perhaps the most challenging responsibility of parenting. It's also a job we can do not by ourselves or in our own strength but only by depending on God. That's why we have come back to prayer—our lifeline as parents—again and again in the pages you've read.

As Rick Joyner said recently, "I have come to believe that all responsibility is beyond human ability. That means that there is nothing we can do right without God. When I think about my family, I could spend all of my time with my wife, or any one of my children, and it would not be enough. In everything we are dependent on the Lord. In all that we have been given to do we must abide in him. If we are abiding in him, which we do by taking his yoke, we actually find rest for our souls, not striving."[1]

I've found that the power to abide in Christ and spiritually parent our children, along with doing all he's called us to, isn't something we can do in our own strength or good intentions, but only by praying for them (and ourselves) and depending on God. And the grace to let them go at the appropriate time, with trust in our hearts instead of angst, emanates from prayer as well. So let me encourage you to commit yourself to being a praying parent—not only when your kids are young and under your roof but also when they grow up, leave home, and have a family of their own. Because there's never a time they don't need our prayers!

And when your children become parents themselves, ask God to make you the kind of grandma or grandpa who will willingly invest yourself in building loving relationships with your grandchildren and passing on a godly heritage.

Now look ahead with me for a moment—what a marvelous thing it will be to see our children someday take the spiritual baton, continue the race we began, and far surpass us in enjoying, loving, following, and serving God. It will be worth every moment we've invested in building the relationship—praying, modeling, having family devotions, teaching them God's Word, and discipling them—to see the ultimate mission accomplished. As we cheer for them from the grandstands of grandparenting, and later from heaven, we'll see their faith firmly in Christ, faces radiant with hope, as they pass on their faith to their kids and grandkids and others around them—until he comes again.

appendix

a **look** at **faith** development **in** children

The following descriptions and theories on faith development in children may be helpful in understanding your child's spiritual journey. While I have not based this book on any specific theory for the reasons explained in the first chapter, it is useful to gain insights from the field of child development as a background to understanding, teaching, and working with children.

Understanding Age Growth

Understanding Age Growth, John M. Drescher (*Seven Things Children Need.* Scottdale, Pa.: Herald, 1976).

Age Five: The kindergarten-age child accepts the fact of God as Creator and loving Father yet at times confuses names and persons of God and Jesus. May worry over ideas that God sees all he's doing. Enjoys stories from the Bible and, most of the time, participating in the Sunday school class at church.

Age Six: To the first grader, God is important; he can accept God's ability to see him, but has difficulty with the fact that he can't see God. When he prays, he expects his prayers to be answered immediately and in a very literal way. Ready for more Bible stories and especially for role-playing them. The six-year-old's ideas about spiritual things are concrete rather than abstract.

Age Seven: The second grader is thinking carefully about God, heaven, angels, and spiritual things. Seven-year-olds can participate in class conversations about abstract spiritual concepts. He loves Bible heroes, and they come alive to him. Has favorite Bible stories and is beginning to make decisions for his actions and behavior.

Age Eight: Since the third grader's world is expanding, he is more interested in missions and in the world. He is beginning to ask questions about things he used to accept on faith. He can read from his own Bible.

Age Nine: The fourth grader has a better grasp of the history of the Bible. He is fascinated with biblical heroes and looks up to them. Teachers who are compassionate and understanding of him can motivate him to Christian character and action. He can understand service to others and has a desire to serve and help.

Age Ten: A ten-year-old can discuss his faith in Christ and is growing more responsive to God and others. He is better able to apply Bible truths to his own life and find meaning in serving and giving to others.

Age Eleven: The sixth grader enjoys group activities at church. He is beginning to think about what he's going to do vocationally in life and needs creative ways to express his faith, to serve, and to relate to others.

Ages Twelve to Fourteen: Since a child in junior high can handle abstract thinking, he can be engaged in some ethical conversations. His questioning about religion should be encouraged and guided. He also needs guidance in applying Christ's work on the cross to his own life.

Ages Fifteen to Eighteen: Capable of deep abstract thinking and deep emotional response to worship, the teen's horizons are expanding. He is thinking about the future and his vocational direction; he is more independent but still needs guidance and dialogue on ethical problems.

Stages of Spiritual Development

Stages of Spiritual Development,[2] Art Murphy, author of *The Faith of a Child* (Chicago: Moody Press, 2000).

The Discovery Stage

A season of constant discovery and exploration in which young children from birth to approximately age seven are constantly discovering new information and soaking up everything in their home environment and the world around them: things they see and experience, parents' and siblings' behavior, Bible stories read to them, church experiences. A time of thinking, observing, processing, and asking questions. These little ones may not understand all the spiritual words they hear at home or in Sunday school, but they are recording it in their amazing memories and may later repeat the words verbatim.

The Discerning Stage

In the kindergarten and early elementary years (approximately ages four to eight), kids ask specific questions, like, "What happens when Grandma dies?" "Where is heaven?" "Can I go there?" "Where does God live?" If they have heard spiritual concepts and Bible stories, they start to personalize them by wondering how it all applies to them. This is the "kick in the womb" stage. The kicks (questions they're asking) aren't necessarily real labor pains, but show that they are beginning the journey and interested in knowing more about God.

Often parents hearing a child's insightful questions think the child is ready for commitment, so they rush ahead and say, "Pastor, I need you to baptize my child this Sunday." Murphy advises, "Life's coming, but it may not be delivery time quite yet." He compares the parents and the children's ministry leaders to pediatricians, but God is the obstetrician. God has our children's spiritual births planned, just as he had a timing for their physical births. Kids may be repeating what they've heard from adults or older siblings, without yet understanding the spiritual terminology, or they may be taking things literally (like the little boy who got a knife from the kitchen and told his mom he was ready to open up his heart and let Jesus in).

While children can have a genuine encounter with God and experience salvation during the Discerning Stage, we can't assume that each child understands the invitation (if your church offers one) at the end of the service and is ready to commit his or her life to Christ. It is important for us to dialogue with the child, listen, pray, and ask God for discernment to gauge our child's spiritual awareness and readiness.

The Deciding Stage

While the most common ages for the Deciding Stage, or making a decision for Christ, is from ages seven to thirteen, it may come at eight, ten, twelve, or in the adolescent or college years. In this season of life, the line is drawn between kids' curiosity and real conviction. In this stage, children begin to understand God's great gift of love, their separation from God because of sin, what salvation means, and then make a decided choice to turn their lives over to God through Christ's atonement on the cross. This is God's just-right time for salvation. The important thing is that it is the work of the Holy Spirit to lead your child to the deciding moment. Our part is to pray earnestly for our children's spiritual eyes to be opened and for their surrender to their Creator, for the ability to answer their questions honestly and to follow obediently the light that God puts on our path in regard to the spiritual nurture of our children. Then we will realize this "right time" for commitment, and it will be cause for great joy!

The Discipleship Stage

The Discipleship Stage of spiritual development begins when your children commit their life to Christ (which could be age seven or seventeen or older) to the time they are truly disciples. It may take a short time to lead a child to make a commitment to Christ, but according to Murphy, it takes about five years to help him become a disciple. The decision is only a beginning—a wonderful step, but a first step. The following months and years are crucial for grounding them in the Bible and in the basic teachings of Christ, teaching and modeling prayer, helping them to connect with God and become anchored in his love, and building spiritual disciplines into a lifestyle of following and serving the Lord.

The Stages of Faith

The Stages of Faith, James Fowler (*Stages of Faith, James W. Fowler: The Psychology of Human Development and the Quest for Meaning*. New York: HarperCollins, 1981).

Since a great part of the modern understanding of spiritual development, in both children and adults, is based on Dr. James Fowler's work, it is useful to review his definition of faith. "Faith is a person's or group's way of moving into a force field. It is our way of finding coherence in and giving meaning to the multiple forces and relationships that make up our lives. Faith is a person's way of seeing himself or herself in relation to others against a background of shared meaning and purpose."[3] Fowler's theories of faith development were based on his research plus the theories of Jean Piaget, Erik Erikson, and Lawrence Kohlberg.

Primal and Intuitive-Projective Faith
(Infancy through Toddlerhood)

Before age two, Fowler describes children's faith as "primal" or "undifferienated" and doesn't actually count or number Stage 1 until the preschool age of intuitive-projective faith. "We all begin the pilgrimage of faith as infants," Fowler says, and this is the crucial time when seeds of faith, hope, and trust are planted, when babies' first images of God come from their parents. "The emergent strength of faith in this stage is the fund of basic trust and the relational experience of mutuality with the one(s) providing primary love and care."[4] At approximately twenty-four months, as the child's language skills take a leap in progress and he begins speaking in sentences, there is a transition from primal faith to intuitive-projective faith, according to Fowler. Spirituality develops primarily through pretend play and imagination during this time. By twenty to thirty months, the child seems to have an image of God, which is a projection of the loving care she has experienced from parents and other adults. God seems to be everywhere because the boundaries between the self and others aren't clearly drawn.

Intuitive-Projective Faith (The Preschool Stage—Stage 1)

Still in the intuitive-projective, (Stage 1) magical stage of thinking, children in Stage 1 begin to ask more questions and develop very imaginative understandings of the universe. A myriad of questions arise: What is this bug for? Who made it? Who made God? Where is he? Why is he invisible? They discover God as Creator from our responses to their many questions. By age four, kids begin to put together pieces of the puzzle from childhood books, Bible stories, pretend play, parents, and peers to make sense of the world around them.

Mythic-Literal Faith (Stage 2)

"The mind of a ten-year-old is an amazing instrument," says Fowler.[5] Instead of a magical, intuitive approach, the ten-year-old is more logical. He works to sort out the real from the make-believe, to develop hypotheses, and to bind his experiences into meaning through the medium of stories. Stories are a primary way of finding truth for the elementary-age child.

Synthetic-Conventional Faith (Stage 3)

Formal operational thinking during the adolescent years emerges with self-consciousness and the ability to reflect. The adolescent's deep hunger "is for a God who knows, accepts and confirms the self deeply, and who serves as an infinite guarantor of the self with its forming myth of personal identity and faith."[6] Others (peers, significant others) have great influence while teens are attempting to become autonomous. A commitment to God during this stage can "exert a powerful ordering on a youth's identity and values outlook."[7]

Individuative-Reflective Faith (Stage 4)

In Stage 4, which moves into adulthood, rituals and symbols are important. People in this stage are forming their own adult structures and life goals. An ideal time for this transition, Fowler says, is late adolescence and early to midtwenties. The person in the individuative-reflective stage of faith asks, "What does it mean?" of liturgical rituals or religious symbols. He begins to take responsibility to work out what he truly believes, not what others around him do, and to docido what he'll base his commitments, lifestyle, and beliefs on. If a person doesn't ask questions and goes unquestioning into a commitment or religious life and then begins to question, ponder, and doubt, it can bring a sense of guilt and great loss (especially if there is great tension with parents or older adults in his life).

Conjunctive Faith (Stage 5)

Conjunctive faith is "a way of seeing, of knowing, of committing."[8] Stage 5, Fowler says, rare before midlife, is a season in which a person appreciates symbols, myths, rituals, and reality. There is a reworking of a person's past, an "opening to the voices of one's deeper self."[9]

Universalizing Faith (Stage 6)

The bearers of Stage 6 faith, whether in the Jewish, Christian, or other tradition, "lean into the future of God for all being."[10] They live in the light and anticipation of the coming reign of God, see the fractures and divisions of the human family with vivid pain, have a sense of "the absoluteness of the divine character" and of inclusiveness of community regardless of denomination or nationalism. They are devoted to "universalizing compassion." They seem "more lucid, more simple, and yet somehow more fully human than the rest of us."[11] As examples of Stage 6 faith, Fowler offers Thomas Merton, Martin Luther King, Mother Teresa, Dietrich Bonhoeffer, and Gandhi.

notes

One–Spiritual Windows: Pathways to the Heart

1. Robert Coles, *The Spiritual Life of Children* (Boston: Houghton Mifflin, 1990), 308.

2. Sofia Cavalletti, *The Religious Potential of the Child* (New York: Paulist, 1983), 24.

3. Karen Henley, *Child-Sensitive Teaching* (Cincinnati: Standard, 1997), 33.

4. Jim Cymbala, *Fresh Faith: What Happens When Real Faith Ignites God's People* (Grand Rapids: Zondervan, 1999), 100.

Two–The Enjoying God Window

1. Sofia Cavaletti, *The Religious Potential of the Child* (New York: Paulist, 1983), 34.

2. Heidelburg Catechism.

3. Bruce Wilkinson, *Experiencing Spiritual Breakthroughs: The Powerful Principle of the Three Chairs* (Sisters, Ore.: Multnomah, 1999), 205.

Three–The Wonder Window

1. Sofia Cavalletti, *The Religious Potential of the Child* (New York: Paulist, 1983), 138–39.

2. Webster's Seventh New Collegiate Dictionary.

3. Rachel Carson, *A Sense of Wonder* (New York: Harper and Row, 1998), 23.

4. Ibid., 67.

5. Rachel Carson, quoted in Miriam Huffman Rockness, *A Time to Play: On Childhood and Creativity* (Grand Rapids: Zondervan, 1983), 133.

6. Terry Willits, *Creating a Sensational Home* (Grand Rapids: Zondervan, 1996), 17–18.

7. Cavalletti, *Religious Potential*, 140.

Four–The Worship Window

1. Ravi Zacharias, *Can Man Live without God?* (Nashville, Word, 1996), 93.

2. Sofia Cavalletti, *The Religious Potential of the Child* (New York: Paulist, 1979), 140.

3. Sonja M. Stewart and Jerome W. Berryman, *Young Children in Worship* (Louisville: Westminster/John Knox, 1989), 13–19.

Five–The Loving God Window

1. Ross Campbell, *Relational Parenting* (Chicago: Moody Press, 2000), 132.

2. Sofia Cavalletti, *The Religious Potential of the Child* (New York: Paulist, 1979), 152–54.

3. Beth Moore, *Breaking Free* (Nashville: Broadman and Holman, 2000), 195.

4. Wes Haystead, *Teaching Your Child about God* (Ventura, Calif.: Regal, 1983), 132.

5. Ibid.

6. Ibid., 136.

7. Ibid.

8. Ross Campbell, *Relational Parenting* (Chicago: Moody Press, 2000), 126.

9. The term "heart wound" is used to describe an injury to the child that causes him to be angry, withdraw, or to put up a dividing wall, in Bruce Wilkinson, *Experiencing Spiritual Breakthroughs: The Powerful Principle of the Three Chairs* (Sisters, Ore.: Multnomah, 1999).

10. Ibid., 237.

11. Kay Arthur, *To Know His Name* (Sisters, Ore.: Multnomah, 1996), 31.

Six–The Bible Window

1. Bruce Wilkinson, *Experiencing Spiritual Breakthroughs: The Powerful Principle of the Three Chairs* (Sisters, Ore.: Multnomah, 1999), 213.

2. Emmett Cooper, *Sweeter Than Honey* (Garland, Tex.: American Tract Society, 1996), 4.

3. Emmett Cooper and Steve Wamberg, *Making God's Word Stick* (Nashville: Nelson, 1996), 78. Emphasis in original.

4. Sonja M. Stewart and Jerome W. Berryman, *Young Children and Worship* (Louisville: Westminster/John Knox, 1989), 22.

5. Ibid., 30.

Seven–The Prayer Window

1. Calvin Miller, *Into the Depths of God* (Minneapolis: Bethany House, 2000), 54.

2. Edwina Patterson, *Praise from the Psalms for Children* (Plano, Tex.: A Heart for the Home, 1998), 11. These praise prayers are paraphrased from Psalms 57–82.

Eight–The Ownership Window

1. Adapted from Lawrence W. Schweizer, *Saying Yes to Jesus: The Next Six Steps in Your Faith Journey 2,* 8 (self-published).

Nine–The Obedience Window

1. Emmett Cooper and Steve Wamberg, *Making God's Word Stick* (Nashville: Nelson, 1996), 3.

2. Greg Johnson, "A Lesson in Grace," *Living with Teenagers Magazine* (December 1999), 9. Used by permission.

3. James C. Dobson, quoted in Draper's *Book of Quotations for the Christian World,* comp. Edythe Draper (Wheaton: Tyndale House, 1992), 459.

Ten–The Church Window

1. Phil Phillips, with Syvelle Phillips, *Helping Your Children Walk with God* (Nashville: Nelson, 1992), 3.

2. Cheri Fuller and Louise Tucker Jones, *Extraordinary Kids* (Colorado Springs: Focus on the Family/Tyndale House, 1997), 225–26.

3. My thanks to Pastor Roger and Lin Story for their consultation on keys to looking for a church.

230 notes

4. David Walters, *Kids in Combat: Training Children and Youth to Be Powerful in God* (Macon, Ga.: Good News Fellowship Ministries, 1997), 6.

5. Phillips, *Helping Your Children,* 189.

6. David Walters, *Parents and Teachers: Equipping the Younger Saints* (Macon, Ga.: Christian Life, 1993), 8.

Eleven – The Joy of Helping Window

1. Bruce Wilkinson, *Experiencing Spiritual Breakthroughs: The Powerful Principle of the Three Chairs* (Sisters, Ore.: Multnomah, 1999), 216.

2. Charles Colson and Nancy Pearcy, *How Now Should We Live?* (Wheaton: Tyndale House, 1999), 415, 487.

3. Ibid., 294.

4. Ibid., 415.

5. McPherson, *Power of Believing,* 50.

Twelve – The Spiritual Gifts Window

1. Adapted from Chuck Swindoll, *Insights Newsletter* 10, no. 7 (July 2000): 2.

2. Miles McPherson, *The Power of Believing in Your Child* (Minneapolis: Bethany House, 1998), 201.

3. Don and Katie Fortune, *Discovering Your Children's Gifts* (Grand Rapids: Chosen, 1989), 19.

4. Ibid., 64.

5. Craig Kielburger, "It Starts with Me," *Guideposts* (November 1999), 3.

Thirteen – The Heritage Window

1. Bruce Wilkinson, *Experiencing Spiritual Breakthroughs: The Powerful Principle of the Three Chairs* (Sisters, Ore.: Multnomah, 1999), 216.

2. John M. Drescher, *Seven Things Children Need* (Scottdale, Pa.: Herald, 1976), 129. Emphasis in original.

3. Adapted from Victor Parachin, "Six Ways to Give Children a Firm Faith Foundation," *The Church Herald,* (February 1996), 26.

4. Lael Arrington, *World Proofing Your Kids: Helping Moms Prepare Their Kids to Navigate Today's Turbulent Times* (Wheaton: Crossway, 1996), 84.

5. Arrington, *World Proofing Your Kids,* 85.
6. Wilkinson, *Experiencing Spiritual Breakthroughs,* 224–25.

A Last Word of Encouragement

1. Rick Joyner, "Trusting and Abiding in the Peace of God" www.morningstarministries.org/Articles/word/aug72000.htm
2. From interviews with Art Murphy, children's pastor at the First Baptist Church, Orlando, Florida. Used with permission.
3. Fowler, *Stages of Faith,* 4.
4. Ibid., 119–21.
5. Ibid., 135.
6. Ibid., 154–55.
7. Ibid., 154.
8. Ibid., 185.
9. Ibid., 198.
10. Ibid., 211.
11. Ibid., 200–201.

Cheri Fuller is a speaker and the author of twenty-seven other books. She won the Gold Medallion Award in 1998, and her best-selling book *When Mothers Pray* is giving moms throughout the United States and the world hope and inspiration to pray for their children.

A seasoned educator who has taught at every level from elementary school to high school and college, Cheri is a contributing editor for *Today's Christian Woman* and writes articles for *Focus on the Family, Family Circle, ParentLife,* and other periodicals. She has been a guest on many radio and TV programs, including *Focus on the Family, At Home Live!* and *Moody Prime Time America.*

Cheri's ministry, Families Pray USA, encourages parents and teachers to raise up a dynamic young generation of pray-ers who know, love, enjoy, and serve God.

Cheri and her husband, Holmes, have three grown children and two grandchildren. Her website (www.CheriFuller.com) features her biweekly column "Mothering by Heart" and resources to raise healthy, spiritual, well-educated children. For information on speaking engagements, contact P. O. Box 770493, Oklahoma City, OK 73177 or e-mail cheri@cherifuller.com.

The songs you sing can shape her musical abilities in the womb.

By age three, she understands thousands of the words you speak.

opening
your child's
nine *learning*
windows

cheri fuller
Formerly titled *Through the Learning Glass*

Your child's capacity for learning is truly astonishing—and you are the teacher. How can you make the most of your incredible, God-given opportunity?

In *Opening Your Child's Nine Learning Windows,* educator Cheri Fuller shares amazing insights into how children learn. You'll find chapter after chapter of principles, brain-building activities, motivation boosters, and practical tips and suggestions to help you take full advantage of nine critical "learning windows" in your child's life:

Music	Language	Emotions
Creativity	Curiosity	Math and Logic
Physical	Spiritual	Values

Punctuated with personal anecdotes and filled with the recent, fascinating findings of research on the brain development of babies and children, *Opening Your Child's Nine Learning Windows* can help you start equipping your child today for a fruitful, satisfying tomorrow.

"Cheri Fuller provides parents with a clear road map for those critical early years by detailing the simple things they can do to enhance their child's learning potential."

—Marianne Neifert, M.D.,
author of *Dr. Mom: A Guide to Baby and Child Care* and
Dr. Mom's Prescription for Preschoolers

Softcover 0-310-23994-X

Pick up a copy at your favorite bookstore today!

We want to hear from you. Please send your comments about this
book to us in care of the address below. Thank you.

ZondervanPublishingHouse
Grand Rapids, Michigan 49530
http://www.zondervan.com